PROMISES AND THREATS BY
ASYMMETRIC NUCLEAR-WEAPON STATES

This book is aimed both at readers with an interest in Promise Theory, who may find here a useful case study, and who may contemplate the development of similar applications in other areas, and at readers who are primarily interested in the political science of nuclear deterrence. The latter readers may then come to an assessment about the usability of Promise Theory as a tool for further work.

Promises and Threats by Asymmetric Nuclear-Weapon States

Jan A. Bergstra

χtAxis press

First published by χtAxis press 2019.

Cover design by Zhaoling Xu.

CONTENTS

PREFACE

Promise Theory as it was designed by Mark Burgess has a focus on information technology and systems design. The use of Promise Theory may be extended, at least by way of a thought experiment, to all subjects where promises play a key role. Threats are similar to promises and a theory of promises plausibly incorporates a theory of threats. Threats play a key role in the theory of nuclear deterrence. In this monograph a survey is given of the role of promises and threats in the context of nuclear deterrence. Particular emphasis is on the role of promises and threats as exchanged between antagonistic nuclear-weapons states with highly asymmetric military capabilities and potential.

The antagonism between the US (United States of America), nowadays a universally recognised nuclear-weapons state and the DPRK (the Democratic People's Republic of Korea, alternatively referred to as North Korea), a de facto, nuclear-weapons state which, however, in some sense lacks universal recognition as a nuclear-weapons state, is put forward as a paradigmatic example of asymmetric conditions.

Manifest asymmetry of military strength is a novel aspect in the context of nuclear deterrence theory when compared with classical nuclear deterrence theory which came about by contemplating the antagonism between the US and the USSR, a conflict which has mainly been perceived as being an antagonism between two sides of essentially comparable military strength.

The antagonism between the US and the DPRK takes the form of an episode in a long standing cold war, the Korean Cold War, which involves in addition to the US and the DPRK, the ROK (Republic of Korea, alternatively referred to as South Korea) and Japan as close allies of the US.

In this monograph the current and potential roles of promises and threats in the military aspects of the Korean Cold War are discussed by way of a case study. This cold war highlights in a most informative manner the asymmetric conditions of a conflict between two nuclear-weapons states. Simultaneously the antagonism between the US and Iran highlights in a novel manner the fundamental battle, as understood by the US, against nuclear proliferation in a phase where proliferation has not yet fully taken place.

Seen from the West North Korea and Iran present two different sides of the coin of non-proliferation.

This book is meant as a contribution to the informal logic of promises, while not providing quantified subjective probabilities, but rather something in between: a way of seeing through assertions to form expectations in an interaction between parties that communicate through promises and threats.

In Chapters 9, 10, and 11 ample speculation is provided on potential application of promises and threats by the antagonistic proponents in case of asymmetric nuclear deterrence. These speculations constitute general explorations, extending beyond the case of the Korean Cold War. These speculations are not meant to relate directly, or even indirectly to the current political context.

Most of the text was written in the last months of 2017 and part of the text can be considered a snapshot taken at the en of 2017. Much has happened since then which has not been taken into account in the text. In particular on several occasions high level negotiations took place between the DPRK and the US which seem to have taken away much of the stress caused by the rather visible crisis in the summer and autumn of 2017, while leaving in the fundamentals of the conflict unchanged, so it seems. The relevance of promises and threats for matters of nuclear deterrence has not changed either by the mere coming to an end of the acute crisis. However, most promises and threads that were issued during this episode may be considered to have expired by and at the occasion of the subsequent high level negotiations. In the final section I will discuss some of the relevant literature of 2018 and 2019.

JAB Utrecht November 2019.

CHAPTER 1

INTRODUCTION

Promise Theory was designed by Mark Burgess, in a series of papers from 2005 onwards, as a way of modelling intent and voluntary cooperation[1]. Although introduced, primarily, as a tool for analysing cooperation in human-machine systems, it proves interesting to apply Promise Theory to purely social and political issues too. The objective of this book threefold, in the order of importance:

- To further develop Promise Theory as a tool for political science, beyond work done in [10] primarily by including threats into the Promise Theory framework.

- To discuss the role of promises and threats in the context of nuclear deterrence, and in particular in the context of antagonism between nuclear-weapons states with a highly asymmetric power distribution and to put forward the Korean Cold War as a unique and perhaps a defining example of antagonism under such conditions.

- To apply Promise Theory for obtaining a better understanding of some recent political events, specifically those of the acute crisis in 2017 (excluding later events), in the unfolding Korean Cold War (KCW).[2]

After some general remarks on nuclear deterrence I will present a survey of the results that emerge from from this work.

1.1 PROMISES, THREATS, AND NUCLEAR DETERRENCE

Nuclear fission was first made a reality by Otto Hahn, Fritz Strassmann, Lise Meitner, and Otto Frisch in 1938, along with a supporting theory in 1939. Leó Szilárd and Enrico

Fermi pioneered nuclear fission based chain reactions in 1942. The first bombs were built under the auspices of the Manhattan Project in 1944.

Nuclear weapons were first used, by the US, against Japan in 1945. That brief episode marked the end of a military conflict as part of the Second World War, and—since then—no other use of nuclear weapons has been observed in a conflict.[3] The number of nuclear weapons in existence has varied enormously over the years. An estimate in 2017 proposed some 10,000 usable nuclear weapons in existence throughout the world[4].

We have no experience of the potential military consequences of using of nuclear weapons in the initial stage of a conflict, and similarly nothing is known by way of experience about the role of nuclear weapons in an intermediate stage of a conflict initiated in a conventional manner. The exercise of power based on the availability of nuclear weapons has been limited since 1946 to the exchange of (conditional) promises and (conditional) threats in which the potential use (or non-use) of nuclear weapons played a role. Due to a lack of historical data, however, the credibility of promises and threats concerning the use of nuclear weapons cannot be assessed in any straightforward manner. Much is known, however, about promises made concerning the non-use of nuclear weapons. Each promise and threat, conditional as well as unconditional, involving the non-use of nuclear weapons seems to have been kept—at least up until the publication of this monograph.

Trust concerning the responsible use of nuclear weapons has grown in the intervening period, both for recognised nuclear-weapons states as well as non-recognised nuclear-weapon states. Living in permanent fear of nuclear war is obviously unpleasant, and the assumption that potential enemies won't start a nuclear war without a convincing reason and justification is reassuring. A widespread consensus thus seems to have grown regarding the credibility of the rationale for the use of nuclear weapons by a nuclear-weapons state: (i) reacting to a nuclear attack by an enemy, (ii) reacting on an invasion or an attack from outside in case conventional weapons will not suffice to defend the state, (iii) reacting on extreme forms of blackmail or extortion by an enemy on whom the threat to use conventional weapons appears not to make much impression.

In connection with the Korean Cold War two additional possible motives for the use of nuclear weapons enter the picture: (iv) reversal of nuclear proliferation and (v) preventing that a nuclear-weapons state develops reliable and modern means of delivery of its nuclear weapons (while having accepted its acquisition of nuclear weapons as an unfortunate event of undesirable though unstoppable further nuclear proliferation). Nowadays motives (iv) and (v) are far from being generally considered adequate justifications for the use of nuclear weapons but that may change in the future.

1.2 THE KOREAN COLD WAR: WHAT IS IT ABOUT?

I will make a simple assumption regarding the core of the conflict that comprises the KCW. This assumption is about the conflict in its recent form, not about its origins in and after the Korean War. The following three assumptions characterise the KCW by highlighting aspects that turn the KCW into a fundamental case in the history and development of nuclear deterrence and nuclear proliferation.[5]

Assumption 1.2.1. *The core of the conflict in the KCW is an antagonism between the DPRK and the US: the DPRK claims the right to be able to defend its integrity against all possible enemies including the US combined with the ROK and Japan, whereas the US is determined to enforce non-proliferation with the DPRK as a major focus of concern.[6]*

Assumption 1.2.2. *The DPRK claims that it has already successfully and rightly acquired nuclear deterrence towards the US, a claim which is not shared by the US.[7]*

Assumption 1.2.3. *The DPRK has become a de facto nuclear-weapons state.[8] The US wishes to convince the DPRK that denuclearisation is preferable. The US considers military pressure to be one of the means needed to achieve the latter objective.[9]*

1.3 A SURVEY OF RESULTS

I will first formulate four Propositions which concisely express the outcome of this work regarding nuclear deterrence:[10]

Proposition 1.3.1. *Promise Theory can be viably extended with an account of threats.*

Proposition 1.3.2. *Promise Theory extended with threats is helpful for contemplating phenomena of nuclear deterrence.*

Proposition 1.3.3. *As long as nuclear weapons have not been actually used in the conflict, promises and threats play a central role in the interaction between antagonistic nuclear-weapons states.*

Proposition 1.3.4. *Higher asymmetry in the power distribution between antagonistic nuclear-weapons states comes with an increased role for promises and threats for the stronger side as well as for the weaker side.*

Moreover, this work is based on the following five assumptions, which, by being validated as a useful point of departure, at the same time also feature as results.

Assumption 1.3.1. *Nuclear deterrence has originally been studied with symmetric conditions in mind, and with the US versus the USSR as a running case study.*

Assumption 1.3.2. *When choosing the antagonism between the US and the DPRK as a case study for the conceptual investigation of nuclear deterrence that is best done in an impartial manner and without "taking sides".*

Assumption 1.3.3. *Nowadays nuclear deterrence under asymmetric conditions requires as much attention as the original case has received, and research on that theme will profit from being studied in the light of a real life case just as well.*

The following two assumptions may be controversial as working assumptions for researchers depending on the political systems in which they are embedded. The very asymmetric conditions of a specific conflict, however, may lead to a high level of tension and uncertainty at both sides which by itself makes it more difficult to take an impartial position when using the conflict as a case study for academic work on nuclear deterrence.

Assumption 1.3.4. *The antagonism between the DPRK and the US can be chosen as an appropriate and convincing running case for conceptual research concerning nuclear deterrence under asymmetric conditions.*

The latter assumption seems to fail on the observation that the DPRK is not a recognised nuclear-weapons state. However, one may consider the absence of general recognition of the DPRK as a nuclear-weapons state simply as an indication and confirmation of the presence of asymmetric conditions.

Assumption 1.3.5. *When choosing the antagonism between the DPRK and the US as a running case study for the conceptual investigation of nuclear deterrence under asymmetric conditions that work can be done in an impartial manner and without "taking sides".*

Assumption 1.3.6. *The antagonism between the DPRK and the US may serve as a running case study for the conceptual investigation of nuclear deterrence under asymmetric conditions, and moreover this "case" may even be considered to constitute a paradigmatic case, (just as the USSR versus the US between 1950 and 2000 has been paradigmatic for antagonism between nuclear-weapons states under symmetric conditions).*

Further conclusions are split in two parts: (i) classifying roles for promises in a political context, (ii) general observations on Promise Theory, and (iii) detailing the role of promises and threats in the context of KCW.

1.3.1   CLASSIFYING ROLES OF PROMISES IN A POLITICAL CONTEXT

In a political context (including the context of nuclear deterrence) promises and threats occur primarily in five different forms;

Concept explanation.

Promises and threats may be used for the definition and explanation of concepts. Example: in Section 6.2 the notion of unilateral nuclear deterrence is proposed, the definition of which uses promises and threats.

Descriptive elements of contracts, agreements, and treaties.

The use of combinations of promises as components of contracts is well-known. Threats may also be used as descriptive elements, (an example is given in Chapter 8).[11]

Military–political status quo capture.

Promises and threats may be used as a formalism for the specification of a specific state of affairs at some instance of time (also referred to as a military–political snapshot or as a military–political status quo).

Example: in Chapter 10 a detailed account is given in abstract terms of possible strategies for both sides in an initially non-violent conflict where one side intends to terminate a status quo of asymmetric mutual nuclear quasi-deterrence, whereas another state intends to stabilise that state of affairs so that it may last perpetually.

Strategy specification.

Bundles of promises and threats may be used for the specification of military strategy. In Chapters 10 and 11 it is outlined how promises and threats may be used for the specification of some military strategies that may pertain to the asymmetric case in particular.

Speech action.

Promises and threats may occur as speech actions (oral or written) for political actors.

Using a systematic perspective on promises and threats may be useful for understanding such speech acts follows:

- by analysing in case of ambiguity the possible meanings of an utterance which is taken for a promise or for a threat.
  Example: in Paragraph 2.3 a survey of possible meanings for a single utterance is given)

- by providing a historic account of such utterances of promises and threats in a conflict,

- by determining which promises and threats are outstanding (that is have not yet been terminated, either kept or unkept), at some moment in time,

- by contemplating or formulating (designing) options for new promises or threats which might be helpful or useful for either side in a conflict to issue. Example: the additional promise mentioned in Section 10.6.

Development of awareness of opportunities and risks.

So-called structural promises and structural threats can be discovered and then phrased as implicit or as explicit promises, thereby becoming part of the awareness of a politician, of a group of politicians, of a state or of a coalition of states.

1.3.2 GENERAL OBSERVATIONS ON PROMISE THEORY

Promise Theory is about communication between agents, with one agent making a promise to another agent as the key primitive. In Chapter 3 below important aspects and requirements on promises will be recapitulated. Here I merely mention the key requirement that promising must respect the autonomy of all agents, including the promising agent, so that a promise made on behalf of another agent can be effective only after the other agent has promised to comply with the promise made by the first agent.

Further development of Promise Theory within this monograph has brought forward the following observations which refine the picture of promises as it had been developed in the setting of Promise Theory in previous works.

Promise Theory can be plausibly extended with threats.

Threats may be considered a special form of promises. It is plausible to consider a theory of threats as a part of Promise Theory at large.

Promises and threats as structured concepts.

It is useful to specify promises and threats with the primary components promiser, body, promisee, and scope, and with the optional components condition and bias as suggested by Promise Theory.[12]

Promises and threats exist at different levels of abstraction.

By including a larger set of features and components the notion of a promise (including threat) gets more refined and less abstract. Depending on the topic on intends to discuss an appropriate level of abstraction (precision) can be chosen. In its simplest form a promise is equipped with a promiser, a promise body, and one or more promisees.[13]

Promises don't create obligations (deontic neutrality).

The core assumption of Promise Theory that (by default) promises do not create obligations unless stated otherwise is very helpful (in the area of nuclear deterrence) and this assumption provides additional expressive power to promises.

1.4　PROMISE THEORY FOR THE FIRST NUCLEAR INTERBELLUM

Since the first phase of use of nuclear weapons in 1945 the world is in a state of nuclear interbellum, a phase between consecutive nuclear wars, and by definition in the first nuclear interbellum. Whether that episode is going to be bounded in time or indefinite is unknown at the time of writing. Once, however unfortunately, a second war involving the use of nuclear weapons breaks out, either locally or on a global scale, the message of this monograph will soon be outdated, or at the least it will be in need of revision. The objectives of this work are limited to an attempt to conceptualise in some detail the current as well as potential forthcoming role of promises and threats during the first nuclear interbellum which has started in 1945 marking the end of WW II.

A second episode of nuclear warfare may or may not take place in the future. If, hypothetically speaking, nuclear deterrence somehow has not worked out the way it has been anticipated and a significant revision of the trust placed in various principles will be needed. In case of a second episode of nuclear weapons utilising exchanges the whole configuration of how promises and threats influence expectations and trust is likely to change at once, and it may change to such an extent that an entirely different mainstream perception of the usage of nuclear weapons emerges.

1.5　COMPARISON WITH OTHER WORK

1.5.1　OTHER WORK ON PROMISES AND PROMISE THEORY

I refer to Bergstra & Burgess [8] for an introduction to Promise Theory and a description of previous work on promises. This work is somewhat informal in comparison to the exposition in [8]. The main difference, between both expositions however, is that this work, like Bergstra & Burgess [10] deals with promises as made by human agents, and more specifically as made in a political context, whereas [8] is primarily, though not exclusively aiming at the use of promises as a means of communication between inanimate agents.

1.5.2　OTHER WORK ON THREATS

An early reference for threats is Baldwin 1971 [6]. The account of threats given below incorporates most advice stated in that paper: (i) threats are are like promises, differing in content rather than in form, (ii) threats must be analysed in the context of an account of promises, (iii) threats (like promises) are too important to be left to game theory, (iv) the lack of a "threat science" is undesirable and politically dangerous. I may notice that I failed to find recent work with a specific focus on threats while previous papers on Promise Theory did not include a discussion of threats either.

1.5.3 CONTRASTS WITH OTHER WORK ON THE KOREAN COLD WAR

Much is written about KCW nowadays because the conflict is active as political conflict. The KCW is a cold war in an unfriendly phase with a risk of spinning out of control. I intend to write differently from the works I was able to inspect in the following manner:

No explicit policy advice.

I do not wish or intend to provide any policy advice for any side of the conflict. Many authors produce suggestions on how to proceed, often aimed at an US centered audience. For instance: Bleiker [14] advices against a confrontational policy from the side of the ROK and the S. Feffer 2017 [23] produces well motivated policy suggestions for the US administration (to enter negotiations), Kaplan 2017 [34] suggest that diplomacy plus deterrence are the only plausible way forward, and sees no reason why nuclear deterrence would not work with North Korea. Stanton, Lee & Klingner 2017 [61] provide rather the opposite suggestion (that the US apply systematic and enduring financial and economic pressure to DPRK). Hewitt 2017 [30] proposes objectives concerning a deal with DPRK, involving a threat with a preparatory invasion of DPRK, which he considers to be advisable. Iverson 2017 [32] argues that a dedicated and internationally united move towards Korean unification may still resolve problems that may otherwise become unsurmountable. Litwak 2017 [36] distinguishes transformational deals and transactional deals, with the Iran agreement being transactional rather than transformational, that difference being the root of US dissent with it, and he suggest that a policy, referred to as coercive engagement, towards a transactional deal with the DPRK is possible and preferable over its alternatives. Litwak's suggestions are quite detailed: e.g.

> The United States cannot and should not offer Pyongyang a security assurance that insulates the Kim family regime from the adverse consequences of increased integration into the international system.

It occurs to me as unproven that inventing new and convincing ways to stabilise and support by way of treaty and agreement the Kim dynasty in North Korea, however foreign to Western democracies it might be to do so, cannot and should not constitute an element of an adequate policy towards the DPRK. In such remarks potentially resides a blind spot for an analysis which is not intentionally impartial. Shen 2016 [57] suggests a phased approach for negotiating with DPRK, first focusing on the so-called three no's:

> no further development of nuclear weapons (including nuclear tests);
> no transfers of nuclear weapons outside North Korean territory; and
> no using (or threatening to use) nuclear weapons

This monograph is neither based on agreement nor on a disagreement with any of these proposals for policy advice. Instead I try to be more explicit, and perhaps creative, about potential options for action, in particular for issuing promises and threats, irrespective of the fact that presenting and discussing such options may be fruitful for either side in the conflict.

Implicit policy advice not used as a motivation.

In some cases the intention to develop policy advice for a specific state, say A, is mentioned as a motivation for research which is so generic that might just as well be used by current or future opponents of A. An example of this style of writing can be found in a famous paper on asymmetric conflict, Arreguín–Toft 2001 [2], who writes, as a part of the motivation (that is how I read it) for his research:

> Second, because asymmetric conflicts ranging from catastrophic ter-
> rorism to military intervention in interstate, ethnic, and civil wars are
> the most likely threat to U.S. security and interests, only a general
> theory of asymmetric conflict outcomes can guide U.S. policymakers
> in their efforts to build the kinds of armed and other forces necessary
> to implement an effective U.S. strategic response.

Simply by speaking explicitly of advice to one side, while not mentioning potential advice to the other side in the same conflict, one cannot claim to avoid that the resulting analysis is also helpful for the other side in the conflict.

I consider this form of symmetry breaking, by claiming to produce unilateral advice, to be unconvincing and I will try to avoid it. Promise Theory is of such a generality that if it is found applicable for one side in a conflict it it is likely to inform the other side as well. It would be illogical to suggest that Promise Theory can, or should, be worked out with a fixed side in mind and in such a manner as to serve the objectives of that side only. It is with emphasising that assessments of a promise or threat are always made independently by a single side (by each side), and that Promise Theory does not rely on the existence of an aggregate ("true") assessment of any promise or threat.

No explanation of past policies.

I will not try to explain or outline past behaviour or current positions of any country, state, politician, or group of politicians. As an example of explanatory literature I mention Sanger & Broad 2017 [53] where an account is given of US cyber warfare directed against DPRK progress in missile development. Instead I will merely try to describe behaviour in terms of promises and threats. By doing so a biased (towards looking through a lens of promises and threats) perspective may result which may be in need of being complemented with other aspects and perspectives before coming to any grounded opinion on policy preferences.

If only because the perspective of promises and threats may lead to biased conclusions, unless balanced by other perspectives, the conclusions of this monograph should not be assumed to translate into policy advice in any naive or straightforward manner.

Classical deterrence theory taken as a point of departure.

I will make use of some viewpoints as developed in classical deterrence theory. In my view theoretical work on the handling of the summer 2017 crisis between the US and the DPRK must take into account the theory of (strategic) nuclear deterrence. For instance Powell 1985 [46] provides a clue on some actions of US President Trump.[14]

No predictions.

I do not try to propose any predictions of future developments, or to propose any assessment of the probability of possible future events or to make any suggestions about an upward or downward shift of the subjective probability of certain possible futures based on past or recent observations.

I will summarise my position on the intended style of writing in three propositions.

Proposition 1.5.1. *Writing impartially (or trying to do so) about the KCW and about policy options all sides involved is unusual. The common form of scholarly work on the subject is either historical, or in terms of policy advice, or a combination of both.*

Proposition 1.5.2. *Classical work on nuclear deterrence, even when stated in terms of US and USSR, has often been neutral thereby striving towards a better understanding of the concept of nuclear deterrence and of the effects that such deterrence may have.*

Proposition 1.5.3. *Just as symmetric nuclear deterrence has been fruitfully studied some 40 years ago, then taking the antagonistic relation between the US and the USSR as a running (if not inspirational) example, but yet in an impartial manner, nowadays it is possible and potentially fruitful to study the role of promises and threats in asymmetric* *nuclear deterrence in relation to nuclear proliferation reversal policies, with KCW as a running example, and to do so in an impartial way.*

1.5.4 RESTRICTION TO EASILY AVAILABLE KNOWLEDGE

Let me add a disclaimer: I have no access to knowledge about military technology which has not reached the public media or easily available journal papers. Access to the literature about military strategy in general and about nuclear deterrence in particular is problematic because a significant part of the literature on nuclear deterrence is protected by pay walls. A pay wall may be unproblematic for a well–equipped and adequately supported professional academic with a well–defined and demarcated research topic, but it constitutes a definite hindrance for a member of the public at large, including myself. Even without this difficulty, the sheer size of the relevant literature renders it problematic to maintain any credible claim of novelty.

CHAPTER 2

THINKING IN TERMS OF PROMISES AND THREATS

In this section I will assume that a promise has a promiser (source), one or more promisees (target), a body (description of what is promised), and a scope, the collection of agents which are made aware of the promise. A threat has a source, a target, a body, and a scope as well. It is assumed that a naive understanding of promises and threats suffices for understanding the propositions and examples of this Section. The scope of promises and threats in the examples in this Chapter is in each case the whole public worldwide, though in some cases restriction to the population of one ore more countries is adequate just as well. Promises and threats in this Chapter have been drawn from news items concerning the KCW in news media from the West. I have made no attempt to investigate the validity of these utterances, working under the hypothesis that these are sufficiently valid to merit attention. In fact each such item may be understood as a promise issued by a an organisation in which the author as well as the readers may have different levels of trust.

2.1 PROMISES, THREATS, AND NUCLEAR DETERRENCE

I will summarise some key aspects of promises and threats in relation to the use of nuclear weapons in the form of a collection of propositions.

Proposition 2.1.1. *From September 1945 till September 2019 (the time of writing this text) all impact of the availability nuclear weapons to nuclear-weapons states has been mediated through the use of promises and threats.*

Some authors view utterances containing more or less clear promises and threats as rhetoric, and then portray promises and threats extracted from rhetoric as a potential danger. For instance O'Connel 2017 [43] considers the US President Trump's rhetoric to be dangerous. By being specific about the role of conditions when extracting a promise from rhetoric utterances such potential dangers can be limited.

Proposition 2.1.2. *In the public perception as well as in corresponding media coverage, the awareness of the role played by conditions in (conditional) promises and threats regarding the use of nuclear weapons is very defective.*

Proposition 2.1.3. *When communicating about promises and threats involving potential use of nuclear weapons often the conditions are left out, thus restricting the focus of attention on the body of a promise or threat.*

Proposition 2.1.4. *The first unconditional promise to make use of nuclear weapons issued by a nuclear-weapons state against a named state (the US and shortly thereafter also Japan) has been issued in September 2017 (by the DPRK government).*

Once, if ever, nuclear weapons are used post WW II that will constitute the second phase of such use. Between first the phase use in 1945 and an eventual (if ever) second phase use of nuclear weapons the role of promises and threats in relation to the potential use of nuclear weapons is essential.

2.2   PROMISES FROM AMBIGUOUS RHETORIC

Public media routinely extract promises and threats from so-called rhetoric as produced by actors in the political arena. However, extracting promises and threats from ambiguous rhetoric is can hardly be done in an unambiguous manner and for that reason it may lead to confusion. As an example, on Twitter 2 January of 2017 US president elect Donald J. Trump wrote:

> NORTH KOREA JUST STATED THAT IT IS IN THE FINAL STAGES OF DEVELOPING A NUCLEAR WEAPON, CAPABLE OF REACHING PARTS OF THE US. IT WON'T HAPPEN!

This utterance definitely counts as rhetoric. It is tempting to understand this utterance as a promise but extracting a promise from it can be done in a plurality of ways. I will discuss several options and I will conclude that the mentioned tweet cannot be understood as a promise in a useful manner. Rather it can be considered as a template from which different promises may be derived, each of which need a check with the author of the tweet before being being advertised as a clarification of "what has been promised".

The utterance is plausibly understood as a promise with as its promiser President Trump, and as a promisee the aggregate agent consisting of the entire US public with the whole world in scope. However, determination of the promise body is ambiguous and leads to a plurality of options, five of which are listed below. I will use North Korea, as used in the quote, instead of DPRK in this listing.

1) **North Korea cannot develop a nuclear weapon able to reach the US.** North Korea won't succeed in developing a nuclear weapon (including delivery technology) capable of reaching (being delivered to) any part of the US.

   (This reading is less plausible as North Korea will definitely be able to drop a nuclear weapon from an airplane if no attempt is made to stop the airplane from entering US territory.)

2) **North Korea cannot develop an ICBM able to reach the US.** North Korea won't be able to develop an ICBM with a nuclear warhead capable of reaching (and then exploding as intended) some part of the US.

   (In this reading North Korea won't be able to master the required technology.)

3) **North Korea will be prevented from developing an ICBM able to reach the US.** The US will insist and enforce that North Korea won't be able to develop an ICBM with a nuclear warhead capable or reaching some part of the US and exploding as intended.

   (In this reading North Korea won't be able to master the required technology. But if needed potentially unlimited military means will be used in a brute force attempt to prevent the DPRK from completing the necessary technological development .)

4) **Faced with an attack by North Korea, US ABM technology is adequate.** Even if North Korea succeeds in building a nuclear weapon which can in principle reach some part of the US, North Korea won't succeed in actually bringing a nuclear weapon into any part of the US. The US guarantees that all missiles sent to it from the DPRK (or from any of its submarines) will be successfully intercepted.

   (In this reading US air defense will with certainty intercept any such missile.)

5) **North Korea will be deterred from a nuclear attack on the US.** North Korea may well succeed in building nuclear weapons which can in principle reach some part of the US, however, North Korea won't even try to make use of such weapons.

   (In this reading nuclear deterrence works as expected w.r.t. North Korea. This reading may be grammatically unconvincing. Though taking that imperfection for granted the reading is peaceful and unproblematic.)

6) North Korea won't even try. In this reading, on the authority of president Trump, North Korea refrains from developing a nuclear weapon able to reach the US. That is North Korea acts as if it has promised not to do so.

(Apart from being implausible, this reading is inconsistent with the autonomy of North Korea, as promises may not be made on its behalf by another agent.)

From this example I infer that it is essential to specify in detail what promise (or threat) is extracted (by whom) from an utterance in advance of portraying that utterance, understood as a promise (or threat), as either sympathetic and reassuring, or as problematic and alarming, or as anything in between.

Proposition 2.2.1. *Sometimes an utterance is labeled in the media as a promise or as a threat, and then qualified in judgemental wordings, without providing the details needed to interpret the utterance as such in a meaningful manner.*

Promise Theory can be helpful for determining which detailed information must be included in an utterance to render its reading as a promise or as a threat meaningful, i.e. to distinguish it from mere posturing or rhetoric.

2.3   EXTRACTING A PROMISE FROM RHETORIC

In September 2017 President Trump wrote (my wording) that the

> "US can and will completely destroy North Korea if that must be done in order to protect the US".

Making use of a plausible, though not specified, informal logic of promises and threats I will take for granted that President Trump has in fact, although implicitly, made, in a single sentence (from which I am proceeding by means of threat extraction), the combination of a promise (in fact an implicit promise) and a threat (in fact an implicit threat). The implicit promise reads as follows:

> "The US can completely destroy North Korea".

which, as a promise, tells nothing new as it is generally assumed that the US can destroy much larger and militarily more potent states than the DPRK, and the implicit threat reads:

Threat 2.3.1. *The US will completely destroy North Korea if that must be done in order to protect the US.*

I will refer to threat 2.3.1 as Trump's implicit complete destruction threat and I will use the abbreviation TICDT for it.

2.3.1   ASSESSMENT OF TRUMP'S IMPLICIT COMPLETE DESTRUCTION THREAT

Some newspaper comments have portrayed TICDT as dangerous rhetoric, as if its meaning were obvious. I have not seen any comments trying to make sense of TICDT. Remarkably it is not straightforward to find out what TICDT might possibly mean. I will look at a plurality of options for its reading.

My conclusion based on this survey of meanings is captured in the following Proposition.

Proposition 2.3.1. *Assessment of TICDT:*

(i) TICDT is a sophisticated utterance,

(ii) TICDT is remarkably ambiguous,

(iii) the most plausible reading of TICDT is the reading specified in Paragraph 2.3.6 below (de facto recognition of the DPRK as a nuclear-weapons state), and

(iv) the most plausible reading of TICDT is peaceful rather than hawkish.

Below I will discuss five possible readings of TICDT in subsequent Paragraphs: (i) a tautology of deontic logic, (ii) a classical tautology by material implication, (iii) an instance of relevant implication, (iv) an instance of so-called "madman behavior", and finally (v) a concealed confirmation that the DPRK is a nuclear-weapons state.

2.3.2   IS TICDT A TAUTOLOGY OF DEONTIC LOGIC?

One may plausibly hold that the "threat" that a certain action will be carried out when it must be done (for whatever reason, including the protection of the US) has no meaning in excess of the logic of "must". It is an inevitable property of an action which both can be done and which must be done that it will be done.

Upon this reading the expectation that TICDT will be kept is 100% as it encodes a a tautology of a deontic logic of action.

2.3.3   IS TICDT A TAUTOLOGY BY MATERIAL IMPLICATION?

One may hold that it is never the case (more precisely, that according to the assessment off each agent involved it is not the case) that "complete destruction of the DPRK must be performed in order to protect the US". The condition being always false the body is immaterial, and the threat will always be kept just as an implication with a false premise (a so-called material implication) will always be true. In this case the threat (promise) becomes a rather trivial variation of a material implication, which must not give rise to any complaints or commotion and cannot introduce additional risks, as its probability of being kept is 100% for logical reasons.

2.3.4 Is TICDT based on a relevant implication?

The interpretation of TICDT, as a tautology of a deontic dynamic logic, as well as its interpretation as a vacuous Promise Theory keeping of which is secured just as the validity of a material implication is guaranteed, may both be considered unsatisfactory, as it may be claimed that by adopting these forms of trivialisation "the real meaning" of TICDT is missed.

Instead one may require that the condition and the promised action are connected in a relevant manner, i.e. that the condition is sometimes true, and by being true the condition explains why the promised action makes sense. So one may focus on an interpretation of Trump's complete destruction threat which coexists with the assumption that in some relevant cases it is true that complete destruction of North Korea must necessarily be achieved in order to protect the US. Now, the latter is not an obvious state of affairs. I will refer to this assumption as the "protection by complete destruction hypothesis".

Definition 2.3.1. *(Protection by complete destruction hypothesis.) The protection by complete destruction hypothesis (PBCDH) asserts that it is realistically conceivable that the complete destruction of the DPRK by US forces is needed in order to protect the US.*

Definition 2.3.2. *(Military–political status quo.) A military–political status quo (in the sense of state of affairs) for a group of states consisting of two or more countries consists of a combination of conditions of military and political nature.*

Any military–political status quo is abstract in the sense that many actual states of affairs may comply with its requirements. For contemplating the reading of TICDT as a relevant implication one needs the notion of a conceivable military–political status quo.

Definition 2.3.3. *(Conceivability.) A military–political status quo is conceivable if it might occur, at least in principle.*

The notion of a conceivable military–political status quo is implicit in the notions of a conditional promise and conditional threat. The conditions of promises and threats are evaluated in a specific military political status quo, while the plausibility or the mere meaning of a conditional promise or a conditional threat is conceptualised by imagining a range of military–political status quo's or even by imagining developments of successive phases of military–political status quo's.

The PBCDH asserts that there may exist a military–political status quo for the US and the DPRK, perhaps involving other countries as well, in which complete destruction of the DPRK is needed for the protection of the US. Such a military–political status quo serves as a witness for the protection by complete destruction hypothesis.

Assuming the PBCDH, it is conceivable that at some stage (in a military–political status quo with some conceivably reachable features) complete destruction of the DPRK by the US is needed for the US to protect the US, and then TIDICT states the obvious, namely that what is needed to protect the US will be done (in the light of the fact that it it can be done).

Understanding TICDT as a relevant implication is not so much problematic and puzzling because of the total destruction of the DPRK it conditionally announces (a disastrous event by any account), but it is rather more problematic because of the underlying idea that the full destruction of the DPRK can conceivably be needed to protect the US. This causal relation between full destruction and protection is hard to imagine, but the above requirements (formulated as promises) seem to provide precisely that state of affairs. In other words the protection by complete destruction hypothesis must be established as a plausible fact. In Paragraph 2.4 below it will be established, as an observation of independent relevance, that indeed the protection by complete destruction hypothesis is valid.

2.3.5   IS TICDT AN INSTANCE OF "MADMAN BEHAVIOUR"?

Madman behaviour is intentional action by a political actor which, according to that actor, may confuse an opponent and make them fear that the situation may run out of control due to the actor's potential irrationality. The actor hopes that madman activity may support the achievement of certain objectives. In view of the casual remark about total destruction of the DPRK as contained in TICDT (and considering such forms of destruction being so grave that casual remarks about it should not be made) one might propose to classify TICDT as a specimen of madman behaviour.

Madman behaviour has been extensively studied in the context of nuclear deterrence and nuclear compellence. A recent contribution to this theme is Sechser & Fuhrmann 2017 [56]. The possibility that TICDT is an instance of madman behaviour cannot be ruled out. However, as Sechser & Fuhrmann indicate, the madman behaviour hypothesis mostly cannot be confirmed in a specific case because that requires looking inside the mind of an actor which is not possible for an outside observer. In a famous historic case involving President Nixon, however, his explanation confirmed that he saw his own action as intentional madman behaviour himself, which is considered conclusive evidence in that matter.

The madman behaviour concept is complex: it ranges from truly mad behaviour (that is the behaviour of a "true madman", however defined), via flawed behaviour (mistaken madman behaviour) and the clever behaviour of an actor impersonating a madman (intentional madman behaviour), to behaviour which has not been intended as madman behaviour in any way but which is successfully portrayed by other observers as being an instance of either true or mistaken madman behaviour (alleged madman behaviour).

2.3.6   IS TICDT MERELY CONFIRMING THAT THE DPRK IS A NUCLEAR-WEAPONS STATE?

Yet another way to look at TICDT is that in classical MAD (mutual assured destruction), say between two states, the whole point is that both states are considered to have issued an implicit promise to destroy the other state when that is the only remaining option in a conflict. The idea of MAD, from the perspective of the US, has been clearly explained in President Carter's Directive 59 (1980) as follows:

> To continue to deter in an era of strategic nuclear equivalence, it is necessary to have nuclear (as well as conventional) forces such that in considering aggression against our interests any adversary would recognise that no plausible outcome would represent a victory or any plausible definition of victory. To this end and so as to preserve the possibility of bargaining effectively to terminate the war on acceptable terms that are as favourable as practical, if deterrence fails initially, we must be capable of fighting successfully so that the adversary would not achieve his war aims and would suffer costs that are unacceptable, or in any event greater than his gains, from having initiated an attack.

TICDT can be read as a less friendly and more concisely formulated version of the same idea.

Assuming that the DPRK is waiting for the recognition by the US that it is a nuclear-weapons state then, in this reading, TICDT comes close to stating just that. If this is the worst threat towards the DPRK to which the US President may commit himself, then that very state of affairs is just what one would expect in the presence of an equilibrium of mutual nuclear deterrence.

2.4   THE PROTECTION BY COMPLETE DESTRUCTION HYPOTHESIS

In this Paragraph I will demonstrate that the protection by complete destruction hypothesis (Definition 2.3.1) is true. This matter is independent of any consideration of TICDT, and it is also independent of any observation concerning the DPRK and the US. It will be phrased in those terms for better readability only.

A military–political status quo will be sketched in which only the total destruction of the DPRK will suffice to protect the US. In other words:

Proposition 2.4.1. *A military–political status quo which serves as a witness of the protection by complete destruction hypothesis is conceivable.*

This proposition confirms the protection by complete destruction hypothesis. The latter confirmation is needed for the reading of TCIDT in terms of a relevance logic as discussed above. It should be pointed out in advance that although the scenario as provided below is quite implausible and speculative, it is not impossible, and that is what matters for the complete destruction hypothesis.

For a military–political status quo to serve as a witness of the protection by complete destruction hypothesis it is required that the following two requirements are met simultaneously.

Sufficiency. Complete destruction of the DPRK can contribute to the protection of the US, and,

Necessity. The US cannot be protected by means of a less (than completely) destructive strike on the DPRK.

Sufficiency is guaranteed in a certain military–political status quo whenever the US is able to perform an effective counterforce strike. That may not be the case at the end of 2017 but it cannot be ruled out that in due time a military–political status quo with such conditions will exist, or that it might have existed had past history been somewhat different.

The requirement of necessity, however, is quite hard to satisfy. At first sight it seems that complete destruction cannot conceivably be necessary in order to protect the US for these two reasons:

(i) Any successful counterforce strike on the DPRK can be performed in such a manner as to reduce the number of civilian casualties, that is in a non-completely destructive mode.

(ii) Even when granting that the threat that the US has a delayed full second strike capability against the DPRK protect (in its capacity as a threat) the US by successfully deterring the DPRK from inflicting a first strike on the US, it is not at all clear how actually carrying out the complete destruction of the DPRK can protect the US against damage that has already been inflicted, in the case that the mentioned threat failed to deter the DPRK from an attack on the US.

In spite of these objections, which would entail that "necessity" cannot apply, i.e. that it cannot be the case that complete destruction of the DPRK is needed to protect the US, I will outline a scenario in which both requirements of sufficiency and necessity are simultaneously met. For that purpose I will now suppose that a military–political status quo is given in the presence of the following combination of additional promises:[15]

1. The US (President) promises that (i) the US will put an end to any (temporary) nuclear second strike capability of the DPRK, and (ii) the US views the complete,

   verifiable, and durable military denuclearisation of the DPRK as a necessity for the long term protection of the US.

2. The US promises to have the capability of a moderately successful (or better) counterforce first strike capability against the DPRK, (otherwise no attack on the DPRK can protect the US).[16]

3. The US promises that it has no successful surgical (i.e. targeting military targets only) counterforce strike capability against the DPRK (otherwise a need to fully destroy the DPRK in order to protect the US cannot conceivably arise).

4. The US promises its expectation that the DPRK will not give in (the DPRK will not denuclearise and and will not bring the development of nuclear weapons to a halt) for less than the risk of its total destruction.

5. The US promises that "in order to make the DPRK change its behaviour the US must threaten it with total destruction".

6. The US promises its expectation that after a nuclear first counterforce strike on the DPRK, both the PRC and Russia would successfully block any further nuclear attack on the DPRK, claiming that such attacks are not anymore needed to protect the security of the US. This promise ascertains that the US can only achieve complete destruction (if it so wishes) of the DPRK in its first strike (even if the first strike could be performed as a surgical counterforce strike).

7. The US promises (in private) to set an example for all rogue states with nuclear-weapons ambitions:

   (i) nuclear-weapons state ambitions are not tolerated,

   (ii) if a state only gives in when threatened with total destruction that is exactly what might happen (not only such a threat may be issued but its keeping by the US must not be ruled out),

   (iii) total destruction may occur even if that course of action is not provably needed for the protection of the US at the moment when it occurs, it may occur with the intention to deter other states from becoming nuclear-weapons states.

Now suppose that in a certain status quo the requirements 1 to 7 are met. One may argue that the DPRK can easily avoid a destructive attack by promising military denuclearisation only *after* a moderately successful counterforce strike by the US has been performed.

   But even if such a promise were made the mentioned military-political state is still a witness of the protection by complete destruction hypothesis. Indeed, in a military–political status quo compliant with these conditions a limitation to a surgical first counterforce strike may not protect the US (so that complete destruction is needed), because the DPRK may not keep its promise (to denuclearise) after a surgical strike (by the US) and subsequently Russia or the PRC may successfully block a second (and destructive) attack on the DPRK, so that the DPRK may retain its nuclear-weapons capability.

The idea is that these conditions are consistent, in the sense that a corresponding strategic status quo is conceivable in principle, and that taken together these conditions create a setting in which the US has no alternative than to perform a completely destructive attack on the DPRK. The objective of such an attack is to deter non nuclear–states from planning to develop nuclear weapons.

2.5   AN UNCONDITIONAL THREAT

Considering the media coverage of the KCW, it is fair to say that an increasing sense of urgency has developed during the summer and autumn of 2017. The clash between demands from the US, the ROK, and Japan on DPRK policy change and the policies, assertions and actions from DPRK side has lead to a regional crisis, which, via the UN Security Council has come to involve the whole world. The promise discussed in Paragraph 2.2 above indicates that US policies are going to change. In this Chapter I will first list some aspects which allow to infer that this crisis has unique novel characteristics, and then I will make an attempt to specify the status quo in the summer of 2017 in abstract terms. I will first list some unique aspects of the KCW during this episode.

2.5.1   UNIQUE ASPECTS OF THE MID 2017 KCW CRISIS

Several aspects of the crisis in the summer of 2017 seem to be new.

Novelty: taking on a nuclear-weapons state. Not before has it been tried to force a nuclear-weapons state, by means of threats involving military options, to give up its nuclear weapons as well as the future development capability thereof.

Thermonuclear weapons are indecisive. The KCW is a conflict about nuclear proliferation involving two antagonistic thermonuclear-weapons states. Not even the (suspected) thermonuclear capability of the weaker side seems to deter the stronger side in the conflict.

Great unknown: can the weaker side endure? It is an open question in the area of nuclear deterrence if a small nuclear power can hold firm against a very strong one when facing a combination of economic isolation, political isolation, financial isolation, and a variety of military threats.

Testing the limits of nuclear proliferation. The KCW crisis is a real life "experiment" regarding the limits of nuclear proliferation expected to have a long standing impact on the future of nonproliferation whatever the outcome is going to be. The KCW crisis seems to be more fundamental than the Cuban missile crisis of October 1962 which was merely about the placement of nuclear weapons under command of the USSR, a state which had to be trusted somehow anyway, as it supposedly had a second strike capability against the US (a state of affairs which retrospectively may be doubted).

Questionable counterforce strike capabilities. Whether or not the US plus the ROK can launch an effective counterforce strike on the DPRK may in fact be be unknown to specialists. The public at large is doubtful about such capabilities, expecting that the DPRK can respond to any attack with a conventional though deadly second strike on Seoul, and guessing that the DPRK already possess IRBM (intermediate range ballistic missile) mediated delivery techniques for a limited number (say 25) of nuclear bombs which might destroy significant parts of the ROK and of Japan.

It's missiles, not nukes. The major structural threat that the DPRK poses to US, the ROK and Japan, transcends its possession of nuclear weapons. It is the systematic and demonstrably successful progress in missile technology, on top of it being a nuclear-weapons state, that makes alarm bells sound.

2.5.2 SEPTEMBER 11, 2017: THE DPRK ISSUES A CONDITIONAL THREAT

On 11 September 2017 a novel state of affairs has arisen:

More UN sanctions against the DPRK proposed by the US. The US has proposed a regime of stronger sanctions against the RPRK.

Triggering the DPRK to issue a conditional threat. In reaction to the proposals from the US the DPRK has issued a conditional threat:

> **Threat 2.5.1.** *The DPRK will inflict great harm to the US in case the Security Council agrees with proposals for stronger sanctions from the side of the US.*

More UN sanctions agreed. On the basis of initiatives of the US the UN security council has agreed (September 11, 2017) with a significant extension of the existing package of economic and trade sanctions towards the DPRK with the intention to move the DPRK in the direction of halting and preferably reversing its development of nuclear weapons systems.[17]

Emergence of an implicit unconditional threat. By its sole condition becoming satisfied the conditional threat "automatically" turns into an implicit unconditional threat.

2.5.3   THE IMPLICIT THREAT BECOMES UNCONDITIONAL

The DPRK has announced in reaction to the agreement of the UN Security Council with the strengthening of sanctions against the DPRK that it will make the US suffer, and inflict damage more severe than the US has experienced thus far. The existing conditional threat had become an implicit unconditional threat.

Threat 2.5.2. *The DPRK will inflict great harm to the US.*

This unique state of affairs may be combined with other observations and questions:

First unconditional threat issued by a nuclear-weapons state to another one.
On September 11, 2017 the weaker side has, explicitly rather than implicitly, issued an unconditional threat to damage the stronger side. To the best of my knowledge this is the first time in history that a nuclear-weapons state has issued an unconditional threat of performing highly detrimental action towards another nuclear-weapons state.

Unconditional threat without time-span.
The unconditional threat as stated by the DPRK towards the US specifies no deadline for its keeping, which may well be a matter of years rather than days, weeks, or months. Nor does it entail any clue on how it might work. Neither does it imply that the damage would be for the US alone, the damage might also be felt by the DPRK, the ROK, or Japan. The threat can be kept in many ways.[18]

The subjective probability of the threat being kept is anyone's guess.
Whether or not the DPRK will keep its threat represents a form of uncertainty about the future which one may specify in terms of subjective probability. It is a matter of assessment which calls for the quantification of subjective probability and which may work out differently for different agents. At the time of writing (September 12 2017) I assign a subjective probability of 5% to the DPRK promise being kept.[19]

The US has already promised full scale retaliation.
Assuming that the blow to the US which the DPRK has announced by way of its threat can be traced back to the DPRK as its cause, that action would represent an act of aggression towards the US, which matters because the US has

repeatedly indicated its intention to respond with full scale military means to acts of aggression.

US retaliation will be tolerated by the PRC.

If the DPRK keeps its threat by performing acts of aggression towards the US, the PRC has promised to stay out of the subsequent conflict, that is not to help the DPRK.[20]

Is there a state of war?

The situation is hard to distinguish from the status quo that would arise (hypothetically of course) after an (unconditional or absolute) declaration of war by DPRK to the US would have been made. The Hague convention of 1907 suggests that "the Contracting Powers recognise that hostilities between themselves must not commence without previous and explicit warning, in the form either of a reasoned declaration of war or of an ultimatum with conditional declaration of war". Threat 2.5.2 may be understood as a reasoned advance warning issued by the DPRK which has not been phrased in the form of a declaration of war. These matters are complicated additionally by the hitherto unsolved problem of the persisting state of war between the DPRK and the ROK since the Korean War ended with an armistice signed July 27 1953 with both sides leaving the task to obtain a peace treaty for future elaboration.

Is threat 2.5.2 known to be a deception?

Roy 2017 [48] claims that the DPRK will not seek war. Although [48] provides an almost compelling rationale for a long term policy of the DPRK leadership, there is no convincing evidence for the US that the DPRK leadership will be as risk averse as Roy suggests.

2.6   THE SECOND HALF OF 2017

During the last months of 2017 important events took place in an almost daily rhythm. Some events may be understood in terms of promises and threats and commented upon accordingly. Here are three examples.

1. On September 23 President Trump indicated (my words) that the DPRK leadership might be near the end of its life-cycle given the aggressiveness of its threats.

2. On September 23 DPRK foreign minister Ri Yong-ho has stated that President Trump's remarks of September 23th as well as an unwanted visit of airplanes amounted to a declaration of war by the US to the DPRK. For that reason the DPRK announced:

Threat 2.6.1. *The DPRK is ready to open fire at any US planes coming close to the DPRK even when not crossing DPRK territory.*

Comments:

   (a) The White House responded by promising that it had not declared war to the DPRK. This response comes with an implicit threat that the US might consider an attack on US airplanes outside DPRK airspace as an act of aggression to which it might retaliate.

   (b) The US (White House) then accepted threat 2.6.1 by promising that such attacks would be a failure, while pointing out the desolate condition of the DPRK air force.

   (c) The White House might alternatively have accepted threat 2.6.1 by means of the following conditional promise (i) there is no state of war, (ii) if DPRK attacks US airplanes outside DPRK territory then the US will launch a counter attack on the attacking forces and systems also when based within the DPRK.

   (d) Threat 2.6.1 constitutes a remarkable suggestion that the DPRK might be willing to engage in a limited military conflict, provided the DPRK is not itself being attacked.

       This willingness indicates an understanding that the US has no options available to initiate limited military operations without taking the risk of full DPRK retaliation while such limited policies for handling the conflict might be needed for the US as well as for the DPRK. Accordingly threat 2.6.1 might conceivably be interpreted as a sign of de-escalation.

   (e) It constitutes a step forward if protocols for limited military action can be developed between the DPRK and the US (and its allies). The importance of such protocols is paramount because the weaker side may plausibly understand and portray its nuclear weapons as a means of deterrence against potentially limited forms of aggression, a strategy which is detailed in Gray 1979 [28].[21]

3. Beginning October US Secretary of State Rex Tillerson indicated the existence of an open communication channel with DPRK leadership whereupon the President openly suggested, by means of a tweet, that talking to DPRK would lead nowhere and was merely a waste of his precious time.

These remarks seem to constitute a promise by the US President not to engage in negotiations. Understanding such promises is simplified by assuming deontic neutrality, i.e. that promising does not create obligations.

4. On October 28, 2017 The Guardian reported some remarks made by US defense secretary Mattis.

> Mattis said the North engages in "outlaw" behaviour and that the US will never accept a nuclear North. He added that regardless of what the North might try, it is overmatched by the firepower and cohesiveness of the decades-old US-South Korean alliance". "North Korea has accelerated the threat that it poses to its neighbours and the world through its illegal and unnecessary missile and nuclear weapons programs," he said, adding that US–South Korean military and diplomatic collaboration thus has taken on "a new urgency". "I cannot imagine a condition under which the United States would accept North Korea as a nuclear power" he said. As he emphasized throughout his weeklong Asia trip, which included stops in Thailand and the Philippines, Mattis said diplomacy remains the preferred way to deal with the North.

Further, again quoting The Guardian of October 28, 2017.

> "With that said," he added, "make no mistake–any attack on the United States or our allies will be defeated, and any use of nuclear weapons by the North will be met with a massive military response that is effective and overwhelming"

The latter part of Mattis' remarks reads as a conditional promise. Now if the DPRK were a recognised nuclear-weapons state this very promise, perhaps implicitly, would come automatically with the doctrine of mutual deterrence for nuclear-weapons states.

CHAPTER 3

A FAMILY OF CONCEPTS FOR PROMISES

Waltz 1978 [65] describes the requirements on a theory: laws are expressions of observed regularities, that is descriptions in words of collections empirical facts, while a theory constitutes an explanation of a collection of laws. Promise Theory, as applied in this monograph, is not considered to be theory in Waltz' sense, as it primarily creates a language of promises without claiming explanatory merit.[22] The latter view of a theory is common in informal logic.[23]

Consistency with the requirements of Waltz might arise if an explanation of observed facts on nuclear deterrence is given by means of a theory which has been phrased in terms of the language of Promise Theory, a promise-theory theory of nuclear deterrence so to say. My discussion will not reach that state of maturity, however. I will merely survey promises and threats as these may occur in the context of nuclear deterrence. Achieving this limited objective requires a theory of promises, in the sense as just mentioned, but doing so will fall short of delivering, as advocated by Waltz, explanations of empirical facts as summarised by laws.

3.1   RECALL AND EXTENSION OF PROMISE THEORY

In this Chapter I will both recall Promise Theory from the original perspective of informatics, and expand it with an account of threats, a necessity when dealing with the phenomenon of nuclear deterrence. More specifically the objective of this chapter is to contribute to Promise Theory in the following ways.

1. To introduce the concept of a promise as a family of interconnected concepts (notions, versions of a notion) linked together by refinement and abstraction. Depending on the intended use in a specific context a more or less refined notion of promise is most appropriate. Refinement of a notion of promise amounts to the incorporation of additional features, while abstraction of a notion of promise amounts to forgetting one or more features.[24]

2. To introduce threats as a refinement (subcategory) of promises.[25]

3. Introduction of the distinction between factional promises (promises of fact) and actionable promises (promises to act).

4. To introduce the distinction between explicit promises, implicit promises (together constituting the operational promises), and alleged implicit promises

    In the context of Promise Theory, promises are by default understood as explicit promises.

5. To introduce the distinction between explicit threats, implicit threats (together constituting the operational threats), and alleged implicit threats.

    In the context of Promise Theory, threats are by default understood as explicit threats.

6. To introduce the notions of a meta-promise and a meta-threat, and to explain communication about implicit promises (threats) and alleged implicit promises (threats) by means of meta-promises (meta-threats).

7. Besides operational promises (threats) and alleged implicit promises (threats) the notion of a structural promise (threat) is distinguished. A structural promise (threat) occurs as the body of a meta-promise or of a meta-threat.

3.1.1   ASSUMPTIONS AND SIMPLIFICATIONS THAT UNDERLY PROMISE THEORY

Promise Theory incorporates several simplifying assumptions, which at the same time serve as criteria for the concept of promise as used and proposed in Promise Theory. These criteria are listed below for the sake of completeness of the presentation and may be skipped at a first reading.

Promising is an action.
Issuing a promise is an action performed by an animate or inanimate agent.

Ground form of promises.

In its simplest and most abstract form a promise is an utterance which has a promiser (also referred to as the source of the promise) performing the action, a promisee or group of promisees (also referred to as the target(s) of the promise) to whom the action (of promising, though not necessarily the promised action, fact, or event, if any) is directed, a body which tells what it means for the promise to be kept, and a scope consisting of agents who are made aware of the promise.

Assertions of fact are considered promises.

A statement of fact as produced by an agent may be understood as representing merely a promise to that extent by that agent. In Promise Theory or writing speaking of facts constitutes a style of communicating promises.

Idempotence.

Repeating the same promise has no additional effect unless the (first) promise has been terminated by having been kept.

Promise Theory as a language for system specification.

A system of cooperating agents can often, usefully but perhaps incompletely, be specified in terms of the promises which each agent is willing and able to issue. Successive and cumulative exchanges of promises underly some fundamental interaction protocols.

A plurality of options for promise body content.

A promise body may pertain to past, current, and future states of affairs as well as to past, current and future actions and events.

Optional causality when a promise is kept.

As an outcome of keeping a promise, as promiser may see to it, or merely expect, that an action is performed or that some state of affairs is obtained, irrespective of the promiser being capable of bringing about that outcome (or being able to contribute to bringing it about) and irrespective of this outcome being considered in any way positive or attractive by the promisee.

Deontic neutrality.

Issuing a promise does not negatively impact the autonomy of any agent involved including the promiser and for that reason promises come by default without obligations for the promiser.

In other words, issuing a promise does not by itself create an obligation, be it a moral, a legal, or a contractual obligation. If an obligation of some kind and with some way of enforcement must be created all of that that should be included in the body explicitly or be included in one or more additional promises.

Subjective necessity of compliance caused by risk of loss of trust.

A promiser (or other agents in scope of the promise) may fear the loss of trust resulting from not keeping a promise so much that a perception of necessity (that is the awareness of a very high priority) results concerning keeping the promise. This sense of necessity is subjective and it is to be distinguished from obligations of any form.

Determinacy.

The meaning of a promise body is supposed to be reasonably clear. Of course this depends on the context but the assumption is that the promisee is satisfied with its ability to figure out what is meant, rather than that the promise triggers extended guesswork about that. For instance if A promises B to pay some amount at some unspecified future instant of time, this body won't qualify as being sufficiently determinate in the majority of contexts.

Promise portfolio.

Agents maintain a portfolio of promises which they have either issued as a promiser or have received as a promisee, or have received as merely an agent in scope. Within the portfolio each promise is followed along its life–cycle.

3.1.2 PROMISE IMPACT CLASSIFICATION

The impact of (issuing) a promise consists of these five components:[26]

Trust dependant adaptation of expectations.

The promisee(s) (as well as other agents in scope of the promise), upon receiving a promise from the promiser will adapt some or all of their expectations. An agent's adaptation of expectations is dependent on their trust in the promiser.

Immediate promiser's bonus creation.

The mere act of issuing a promise may by itself be rewarding for the promiser. The reward is likely to be positive but it may be negative as well.[27]

Immediate promisee's bonus creation.

The mere event of receiving a promise may by itself be rewarding for the promisee or for some of the agent in scope of the promise. Different agents in scope may experience quite different bonuses. The reward may be negative as well as positive for an agent in scope.

Promise life–cycle startup.

Upon being issued, a promise sets in motion a promise life-cycle running inside each agent in scope of the promise, all of whom may monitor to what extent the promise is being kept. Different agents may terminate this life-cycle at different instants of time and for different reasons. During the life-time of the promise agents in scope make one or more assessments of the subjective probability of the promise being kept. Upon termination of the promise life–cycle, (either by the promise being assessed as having been kept, or by it becoming clear that the promise has been withdrawn or that it is not going to be kept) a final assessment takes place.

Trust update.

Depending on its assessment of the promise being kept the promisee (as well as other agents in scope) will adapt their trust in the promiser. Trust update may occur initially after receiving the promise and may occur in later phases repeatedly as a side effect of successive assessments of the same promise.

3.1.3   MOTIVATING DEONTIC NEUTRALITY

The reasons for requiring deontic neutrality for promises as well as for threats, are these:

Principle of agent autonomy.

Agents are supposed to be autonomous as a matter of principle and agents must not violate the autonomy of other agents by issuing a promise. As a consequence in the presence of conflicting promises, it's up to the promiser to determine how to proceed, in particular not to keep at least one of both promises. Stated differently, due to deontic neutrality, there may only arise tradeoffs between promises that can't be kept at the same time.

Avoidance of conflicting obligations.

An agent cannot solve the problem posed by conflicting obligations, not even if the agent has created these obligations all by itself. If obligations are created, for instance as a side product of issuing promises, the origination of conflicting obligations can not be avoided in a plausible manner. As a consequence by allowing promises to create obligations promises will become much less useful as a tool for distributed self–organisation in agent communities.

Obligations as an optional feature.

Promise Theory is primarily meant as a tool for the requirements capture and for interaction design in the context of cooperating artificial agents. For that reason there is a need to have Promise Theory available without any mention of ethics or morality.

By allowing a promiser to accept a moral (or legal, or contractual) obligation, if and only if the body of the promise, makes explicit mention of both the existence of an obligation and of it being accepted by the promiser the feature of obligations can be introduced in a Promise Theory based system specification.

Is assumed that for use in a political context the assumption of deontic neutrality is just as useful as for use in the context of communities of artificial agents, which has been the original context for Promise Theory.

The virtue of deontic neutrality is summarised in the following Propositions.

Proposition 3.1.1. *(Deontic neutrality.) By issuing a promise (including threats) a promiser does not automatically impose on itself any obligation. If the promise body explicitly includes assuming an obligation then, once the promise has been accepted by the promisee (by way of a reciprocal promise with the original promisee as a promiser) an obligation for the promiser has been created.*

Proposition 3.1.2. *Deontic neutrality guarantees that while promisers may be confronted with conflicting promises thus being required to choose which promise to keep, promisers are not confronted (as a consequence of their history of issuing promises) with the unsolvable dilemma resulting from conflicting obligations.*

3.2 META-PROMISES AND IMPLICIT PROMISES

A meta-promise is a promise about a promise or about a threat. If A issues promise p to B then C may issue the meta-promise "A has issued promise p to B" to say D. Every promise p as described in this monograph may be understood as a shorthand of a meta-promise by the author to the reader reporting that promise p has been issued. Facts (assertions of fact) may be understood as meta-promises as follows: "fact f" (as mentioned in a text by author A) abbreviates "A promises f to the reader".[28]

3.2.1 IMPLICIT PROMISES

An implicit promise is a promise which, though not conveyed by way of an explicit utterance is assumed to be created (bay way of association, and possibly involving assessment) from an agent's behaviour.[29] Every implicit promise has an explicit version, which, however is unlikely to be issued. Implicit promises are created from behaviour and from rhetoric by means of promise extraction.

When speaking of this implicit promise it is useful to imagine a spectator who issues (utters) the meta-Promise Theory that the "seller has promised to sell the (mentioned) item to the customer". An implicit promise is assumed to be uncontroversial in that the promiser of the implicit promise is prepared to behave as if the explicit version of it had been issued (by the promiser). However, given an implicit promise p, one may imagine that another agent promises that it "has noticed the promise p having been made, though in an indirect manner".

3.2.2 ALLEGED IMPLICIT PROMISES

A Promise is extracted from rhetoric or from behaviour may fail to capture its promiser's intentions. In such a case promise extraction produces what I will call an alleged implicit promise. As with implicit promises it is plausible to assume that alleged implicit promises are communicated via meta-promises.[30]

3.3 STRUCTURAL VERSUS OPERATIONAL PROMISES

It is common to speak of the promise of quantum computing and the promise of machine learning and similar promises which are implicit in a societal trend rather than having been explicitly included in the body of a promise by a promising agent.

I will speak of a structural promise if the term promise is meant to represent a positive outlook for a bundle of potential further developments. Such developments may range from technology to politics, and may be morally judged in different ways. An operational promise instead is a promise viewed as an action (utterance) performed by an agent, or as an implicit promise attributed to that agent.

A more precise description of operational promises is given below. By default I will refer to an operational promise as a promise. Thus instead of the promise of quantum computing I would prefer to speak of the structural promise of quantum computing in case some ambiguity might arise. Structural promises capture (expected) emergent properties of systems and developments. Structural promises are discovered, observed, or claimed rather than issued or made.

By forwarding a well-known structural Promise Theory trust by other agents in scope in the the forwarder need not be at stake as in most cases the time span needed to make an assessment about the structural promise being kept is far too long anyway.

Once a structural promise has been discovered and communicated, it may be turned into an explicit promise by any agent. The main consequence of a promise having been turned (or rather cloned or copied) into an operational promise is that promiser and promisee are now specified and side effects on trust in the promisers become major side–effects.

Structural promises are objective in the sense that scientific research may reveal or discard structural promises. Structural promises may be hypothesised and may be the subject of extended disputes by experts coming from different backgrounds and using different approaches. There is a gradual transition from explicit promises to structural promises. In principle one can forget about structural promises by always viewing the agent who forwards a structural promise as its promiser.

Just as implicit promises and alleged implicit promises, structural promises are plausibly communicated by a forwarder as a component of a body for a meta-promise.

3.4 FEATURES OF OPERATIONAL PROMISES

In order for promises to play the role of operational promises the notion of a promise as used in a specific application context is supposed to be characterised and thereby restricted by the collection of features, including the ground features, which are made use of in the application at hand. Thus by making use of more features a more refined notion of promise is obtained, while by making use of smaller feature collection a more abstract notion of promise is obtained.

This Section provides a comprehensive survey of features for promises.

3.4.1 GROUND FEATURES

All promises have at least these four features, also referred to as ground features:

Promiser.

>Each promise has a promiser, that is an agent who issues the promise,

Promisee.

>A promisee, that is an agent to which the promise is primarily directed. The promisee may be an aggregate agent in which case one may also speak of a collection of promisees.

Scope.

>A scope consisting of one or more agents (at least including the promisee or promisees) who take notice of the promise being issued. Agents in scope of the promise maintain a record about the promise which is used for updating its status, as perceived by the agents, when following a trajectory though its life–cycle (see below).

Promise body.

>The body specifies the content of what is promised. Issuing a promise amounts

to the production and distribution of a documented intention as specified by the promise body. A promiser may in fact not intend to keep a promise, in which case the promise is a deception (on top of being a promise).

3.4.2 FEATURES FOR CONDITIONS AND TIMING

Time–span.

After the time–span has elapsed the promise terminates whether or not it has been kept. The time–span may be unbounded.

The time–span may be viewed as an aspect of the life–cycle shared by all agents involved in the promise.

Condition(s).

A promise may be conditional, if so it has one or more conditions, where a list of conditions is understood as a conjunction of these. A condition may be any action or state of affairs (including the keeping of another promise).

Upon a condition being satisfied and that fact becoming known to an agent maintaining a record of that promise, the promise (or rather its record) is transformed into a promise with fewer conditions, upon it being refuted the promise is rendered vacuous and terminates for that reason. Once each of the conditions has been assessed as having been satisfied the conditional promise, as represented in an agent's life-cycle bookkeeping for that promise is transformed into an unconditional promise.

Single conditional (promise).

For promises with a single condition some additional features are provided. It is required that any condition once becoming true will stay true until the promise expires.

Positive conditional (promise).

If the condition is met the body is supposed to be complied with.

Deadline on condition.

For a positive conditional promise with a single positive condition the (optional) deadline indicates that after expiration of that duration, if the condition is not yet met, the promise expires and is understood as having been kept. An optional deadline for a positive conditional promise is provided then this replaces (overrides) the time–span if present.

Negative conditional (promise).

For a negative conditional promise with a single condition a deadline must be provided, the deadline indicates that after expiration of that duration, if the condition is not yet met, the body of the promise must be complied with.[31] The deadline on condition in the case of a negative (single) conditional promise is the same as its time–span, if present.

Deadline for effectuation.

Besides a deadline on the condition, a deadline for the effectuation of the body upon the promise having been challenged (either by its positive condition becoming true, or by its negative condition not becoming true at the end of the deadline on condition) may be provided. A deadline for effectuation facilitates the provision of a systematic assessment whether the promise is being kept or not.

3.4.3 EXTERNAL FEATURES

External features provide various forms of labeling meant for external reference.

Label (alternatively: Name).

When writing about promises is is useful to provide a promise with a label that serves as a name subsequent referencing. Labels (names) are invariant during the life-cycle and for each application of Promise Theory names are supposed to be unique.

Kind.

A promise is of the first kind unless it is of the second kind. A promise is of the second kind if the promiser issues a promise to act as if another agent had made a promise, or if the promiser asserts that it will act as if a promise were made to another agent than the promisee, or both. I refer to Bergstra & Burgess 2014 [8] for more detail on kinds of promises. In the current monograph only promises of the first kind are used or discussed.

Promise bias.

Optionally a promise may be understood best in the context of a bias held by the promiser concerning certain point of view or objective.[32]

Claim.

The claim of a promise is a description of the state of affairs which is achieved upon the promise having been made. The claim can be used to communicate the objective of issuing the promise.[33]

Immediate promiser's bonus.

A promiser may by the mere act of issuing a promise experience a positive or negative bonus. For instance issuing the promise to visit a friend may make the promiser feel better (due to a positive bonus), quite irrespective of the promise being kept.

Immediate promisee's bonus.
A promisee may by the mere event of receiving (or being witness to the issuance of) a promise experience a positive or negative bonus. For instance receiving the promise from a friend that they will pay a visit may make the promisee feel better (due to a positive bonus), quite irrespective of the promise being kept.[34]

Agent animacy
Promises and threats may be categorised according to whether or not promiser and promisee(s) are animate. Four types of promise result. I provide some explanatory comments for this ramification of promises.

Artificial agent to artificial agent.
This is the most ubiquitous case in informatics, e.g. a website host promising a bot to deliver a web page in return for a registration. The bot accepting that promise by engaging in the requested registration.

A virus contained in a document provides a promise (to render a document in an orderly manner) which is at fault so that the promise is a deception.

Artificial agent to human agent.
This case has come to prominence with ransomware. An infection with ransomware of a host may be considered as the confrontation with an artificial agent which, after entering a system and encrypting important data found on that system makes two promises to the users of the host: (i) upon receiving a specified payment before a given deadline the data will be decrypted (or a key for doing so will be provided), and (ii) in the absence of the required payment the decryption can't be undone anymore.

For a human agent the question is whether or not to accept the first promise by making the required payment. This is hugely a matter of trust: making the payment is futile if there is no expectation that the data will be decrypted.

A common case of an artificial to human promise is found when an app promises access upon registration conditional on confirmation of the intention to access via another communication channel (SMS, WhatsApp, email etc.).

Human agent to artificial agent.
Technically such promises take the form of artificial agent to artificial

agent(s) where receiving artificial agent(s) acts as proxy (proxies) for a human agent.[35]

Human agent to human agent.

Such promises are central to any branch of business. Some examples:

- The promise made by a service provider to a client for regularly upgrading the software in order to comply with regulation regarding data protection and data integrity.

- The promise made by a software provider that unless an upgrade is installed before some deadline the client will be in breach of a national regulation on data protection.

- The promise made by a hardware vendor that a laptop which he is selling will still work well and without loss of data after having been submersed in salt water for at most 24 hours.

It is assumed that if the promisee is animate so are other agents in scope, and with a inanimate promisees come inanimate agents in scope.

3.4.4 PROMISE QUALIFIER FEATURES

Qualifiers provide a typing of promise bodies.

Documented intention (actionable promise).

The promiser claims a causal and active role in bringing about the expected state of affairs.

These are the promises of the first kind in [8]. Documented intentions (as promises) are also called actionable promises.

Acceptance of documented intention.

The promiser accepts the promise made to it (as a promisee) by an agent (in the role of an original promiser) and renders this acceptance as a promise made to the original promiser.

Acceptance is also possible for a threat: the promiser acknowledges and thereby accepts the existence of a threat as issued by the promisee.

Rejection of documented intention.

The promiser indicates unwillingness to accept the promise made to it (as a promisee) and renders this rejection as a promise made to the original promiser.

Documented expectation.

The promiser claims no causal role in bringing about the expected state of affairs (expectational promise).

These promises correspond to promises of the fourth kind in [8] provided one accepts the existence of an agent which may bring about the expected state of affairs. A documented expectation promise results from a promise of the fourth kind by abstracting from the latter agent. Documented expectations are weaker than documented intentions because the promiser outsources any responsibility for keeping the promise.

Agreement with documented expectation.

The promiser promises agreement with an expectational promise to the promiser of the latter (acceptance of expectational promise.)

Rejection of documented expectation.

The promiser indicates disagreement with original promiser's expectation cast as a promise to the latter (rejection of expectational promise.)

Promise qualifiers are alternatively referred to as promise types. When denoting promises in structured notation, as in Bergstra & Burgess 2017 [10] or in symbolic notation as in Bergstra & Burgess 2014 [8] the following signs are used to indicate qualifiers:

- documented intention: +;

- acceptance of documented intention: −;

- rejection of documented intention −!

- documented expectation: [+];

- agreement with documented expectation: [−];

- rejection of documented expectation [−!].

Documented expectations (as promises) are alternatively called promises of fact. A promise of documented expectation is also called a promise of fact. Several cases are distinguished for promises of fact, which also serve as promise qualifiers:

Promise of current fact.

The default meaning of promise of fact indicates that the promise asserts the truth of a statement though presented as a fact. Promising a (current) fact is a preferred method for distributing fake news.

Promise of historic fact.

Assertions about the past are a special case of promises of factual promises. Historical fake facts are spread in the same way.

Promise of future fact.

A promise of a future state of affairs comes close to a prediction.

Promise of scientific fact.

A promise of fact together with the Promise Theoretic scientific evidence has been found for the "fact" constituting the promise body.

Promise of alternative historic fact.

A promise asserting a past state of affairs which is intentionally deceptive.

Promise of future alternative fact.

A deceitful promise asserting the expectation of a future state of affairs.

Subjective probability according to the promiser.

To any promise of fact the promiser may assign a subjective probability. The subjective probability may either be private (only known to the promiser), or semi-private (only known to promiser and the promisee(s), or public (also known to all agents in scope).

Facts, when proclaimed by means of an utterance unavoidably degrade into promises of fact which typically cannot easily be distinguished from alternative facts (i.e. promises of alternative fact). In ordinary discourse a speaker will label some promises of current fact (historical fact, future fact) simply as historical facts, current facts, or expected states of affairs. For a promise of fact some form of consensus mechanism may be used to find out if it can be elevated to the level of a promise of scientific fact or of it ought to be degraded to the level of a promise of alternative fact, or merely to the level of a mistaken promise of fact, or even to the level of a promise of fact based on mistaken science.

3.4.5   PROTOCOL FEATURES

As a feature for a promise a protocol for how an agent may be dealing with a promise once received may be included. Multiplicity of promiser and promise is also considered a protocol feature.

Decomposition of aggregate agents as promisers.

An aggregate of agents may also be considered an agent (for more information see the compound agents as put forward in Burgess 2014 [17]). If an aggregate agent issues a promise, if one of those agents fails to keep its part of that promise, such failure is only moderately held against the other agents in the aggregate. In other words a promise issued by a group amounts to little more than (i.e. decomposes into) a combination of promises of its constituent agents. If an agent in an aggregate agent wishes to promise one or more other agents in the same aggregate will indeed keep their part of the promise such promises must be included explicitly in the promise body, or in the form of additional promises. As a feature the aggregate agent feature explains how the promiser can be seen as an aggregate and to which extent the promise can be decomposed into components each of which are promises issued by single agents or by smaller aggregates of agents.

Promise life–cycle.

A promise moves through a life–cycle. More specifically each agent in scope of the promise maintains a copy of it which moves through its own life-cycle. A (copy of a) promise may terminate by being kept, being (explicitly) not kept, being withdrawn, and by being forgotten. Agents in scope of the promise maintain a record of it which serves to store the state of the promise it its envisaged life–cycle.

Promise assessment protocol(s).

Assessing whether or not, and to what extent, a promise is kept, is a matter for each agent in scope of the promise, indeed such assessment for the same promise may vary between different agents, (also in case these agents understand the promise to be at the same stage of its life-cycle). If a conditional promise depends on the assessment of the fate of another promise different agents may hold different copies of the original conditional promise in their collection of incoming promises.

3.5   ABSTRACTION AND REFINEMENT OF NOTIONS OF PROMISE

Give the survey of promise features each subset of the listed features including all ground features gives rise to a notion of promise. This phenomenon is captured in two Propositions as follows.

Proposition 3.5.1. *A notion of promise (alternatively: a version of the promise concept) is given by a subset F of the collection of features which includes the ground features. Instances of that notion for a given F are called F-promises.*

Proposition 3.5.2. *If G extends F then (i) G-promises are refinements of F-promises, (ii) F-promises are abstractions of G-promises, and (iii) F-promise is a more abstract notion of promise than G-promise and G-promise is a more refined notion of Promise Theoryan F-promise.*

3.6 COMMENTS ON THE LISTING OF PROMISE FEATURES

This list of features serves as a description of the concept of a promise, or more specifically of a range of notions of promise parametrised by subsets of the set of features. Determinateness is an uncommon criterion, and decomposition of aggregate promisers is not taken into account. Determinateness has been included as a requirement in order to be able to better differentiate promises from threats.

Defining promises by means of the criteria listed in Paragraph 3.1.1 and parametrised by subsets of the features listed in Paragraph 3.4 deviates from the colloquial use of the term. Gerring 1999 [26] discusses in detail how concepts may be formed in the case of social sciences. In the light of intended applications to political science it is justified to contemplate the concept of a promise, as it conceived in Mark Burgess' Promise Theory, from the perspective of concept formation in social sciences.

Gerring indicates that deviations of conventional meaning need not necessarily lead to the use of different terms or the formation of neologisms, and I will assume that this guidance applies in the case of promises. Further Gerring suggests that a good concept can be identified by virtue of eight qualities of it: familiarity, resonance, parsimony, coherence, differentiation, depth, theoretical utility, and field utility. The given definition of promises provides adequate differentiation from related concepts such as: deception, threat, obligation, and imposition. This differentiation goes at cost of parsimony understood as the brevity of a term or phrase as well as of its definition. Gerring acknowledges that defining concepts is a matter of trade-off. Whether or not Promise Theory conceptualises promises in such a manner that a good score on Gerring's criteria is obtained remains to be seen.

CHAPTER 4

PROMISE THEORY EXTENDED WITH THREATS

A (conditional) threat is a (conditional) promise, which in addition meets the following five additional criteria:

Promisee's disadvantage.

> The body of the promise outlines a state of affairs (or an action, or a process, or a development) which, when becoming a reality (i.e. when kept), according to the assessment of the promiser is detrimental for the promisee(s). In other words a threat promises a negative outcome to its target.

> There are exceptions to this requirement. An agent in the scope of a promise may label the promise as a threat even if the source of the promise is not intending to promise a negative outcome for the target. A promise is a threat as well if a significant majority of agents in scope considers it to be a threat.

Uniformity of assessment.

> According to the assessment of the promisee it is plausible that most observers (including the promiser) would agree with the classification of the keeping of the body of the promise as being detrimental for the promisee (as well as perhaps for other agents possibly including the promiser). In other words: there is ample consensus on the negative value to target.

Uncertainty concerning intention of source and meaning of body.

> The specification of what it means that the promise is kept, i.e. the body of the promise, is to some extent unclear and uncertain, thereby leaving the promisee

and other agents in scope of the promise (threat) puzzled about what exactly is to be expected. In other words: the requirement on determinacy that is assumed for promises is weakened for threats and the source may indicate uncertainty about its intention to keep the promise, or may indicate a lack of information about the promised action or state of affairs.

Quantified subjective probability of keeping for source.

Instead of determinacy the quantification of subjective conditional probability (of the body of the threat coming true upon possible conditions being met) is required. This quantification may be provided with rational numbers but also with labels for probability ranges. (In the absence of any quantification the threat amounts to a mere assertion of risk). The subjective probability must be known to the source, whereas it may be unknown for the receiver to the threat targets and other agents in scope.

Strong deontic neutrality w.r.t. the target.

A threat won't oblige the source to anything w.r.t. the target. Accepting an obligation to keep the threat cannot be explicitly included in a threat either (as it might be in a promise).

Weak deontic neutrality for promises merely indicates the absence of any obligation unless specified explicitly. Strong deontic neutrality rejects any construction of an obligation from a threat. Such an obligation can only be cast in terms of an additional promise (by the source of the threat) to accept the obligation.

A threat may, in the eyes of the source, at the same time constitute a promise to other agents. Any obligatory aspects need to be obtained by means of additional promises which make explicit mention of such obligations, however.[36]

It is difficult to capture the distinction between promise and threat precisely. The borders between these notions are likely to differ for different agents and in different circumstances, in other words it will be up to an agent's private assessment to make that distinction.

For a promise it is not required that there is a positive value to target. Each threat is a promise as well, but not conversely. A threat is deceptive if the subjective conditional probability (for the source) of it being kept (upon the conditions of the threat, if any, having been met) is low.

A threat may be valued differently by its target and other agents in scope. For instance a Promise Theory a (known but still free) thief will be jailed (a promise made to the thief) when detained may be considered positively by a community (scope) but nevertheless is a threat. A promise to imprison that person without due process may be regarded negatively by those persons in a community who prefer due process over revenge. A promise to award the thief instead with a prize is likely to be regarded negatively by the agents in scope but is not considered a threat as it, i.e. the effectuation of its body, is positive towards the promisee.

4.1   THE FEATURES OF THREATS AS PROMISES

Threats being promises makes threats into a subclass of promises using the terminology of object-oriented design. Thus threats inherit the catalogue of possible features listed for promises above, and with the same features as ground features.

As it is the case with promises, subsets of the possible features for threats serve as actual parameters for tailor made notions of threat with smaller sets of features corresponding to more abstract versions of the concept of threat.

4.1.1   ADDITIONAL FEATURES FOR THREATS

As a subclass of promises, threats may have additional features, that is features which are more plausible for threats in particular than for promises in general. I will now list some useful additional features for threats. I will make use of several features specific for threats[37]

Relative cost.

Relative cost expresses the cost for the source when putting the body into effect. Relative cost is given by a rational number in the range $[0, 1]$. Relative cost is a normalised measure taking the totality of potential threats into account.

Negative impact.

Impact expresses how detrimental putting the body into effect is for the target(s). Impact is given by a rational number in the range $[0, 1]$. It is assumed by way of simplification that impact is the same from the perspective of all agents involved.

Source credibility.

Intended source credibility is given by a rational number in the range $[0, 1]$. It expresses the subjective probability assigned by the source to its keeping the threat upon it being challenged (the condition(s) having become satisfied). Source credibility is a private attribute of the threat. It is known to the source but not communicated to the target and to other agents in scope of the threat as a part of the utterance of it.

Intended target credibility.

Intended target credibility is the subjective probability which the source intends (aims at) the target(s) to assign (upon receiving the threat) to the source keeping the threat. Like intended source credibility the intended target credibility is a private attribute for the source.

4.1.2 THREAT SIGNIFICANCE

It is tempting to quantify the strength of a threat. I will propose some measures for threats: significance, credibility ratio, and effectiveness. I will first discuss threat significance.

By combining cost and impact the significance for the target(s) of the threat being kept may be measured. Significance measures the degree to which the source of a threat turns a capability into a serious risk for the target, while being unexpectedly insensitive for the consequences of keeping the threat for themself.[38]

Definition 4.1.1. *(Significance.) For a threat equipped with the features relative cost (c), measured as a fraction of the wealth of the source, and relative impact (i) measured as a fraction of the wealth of the target, its significance (s) is given by the the product of the ability (a) of the source to keep the threat, measured as a number in $[0, 1]$, relative cost, and the relative impact: $s = a \cdot c \cdot i$.*

The issuing of a threat with $a > 0.5$ and $c > i$ may signal desperation from the side of its source. The significance measures what is at stake.

4.2 THREAT CREDIBILITY

A conditional threat involves a condition C such that once, according to the source, C happens to be satisfied, the source has promised to see to it that state of affairs as specified in the body of the threat will be put into effect. Typically a condition may take the form of "an event in a class C_e of events has occurred since the threat has been issued".

I will use an adaptation and extension of the structured notation for explicit promises of Bergstra & Burgess 2017 [10] as a structured notation for threats. The mentioned structured notation for promises is extended with the option to list private features, that is features known to the source only. In this case source credibility and intended target credibility are included as private features.

4.2.1 STRUCTURED NOTATION FOR CONDITIONAL THREATS

Now a conditional threat may be denoted as follows:

> **name** n
>
> **source** S

body B

target T

positive condition C

(private) source credibility $p = P_S(C, B)$

(private) intended target credibility $q = P_T^i(C, B)$

scope V

For conditional threats I will make use of the following technical definitions.

Definition 4.2.1. *A conditional threat is challenged when and if its condition becomes valid.*

A threat which is never challenged (i.e. which is not challenged before expiration of its time-span) is kept by default.

Definition 4.2.2. *The source credibility, $P_S(C, B)$, of a conditional threat is the subjective conditional probability that the source (promiser) assigns to body B coming into effect if it is challenged , i.e. once C happens to have become valid.*

Definition 4.2.3. *The intended target credibility, $P_T^i(C, B)$, of a threat is the subjective conditional probability that the source hopes (intends) the target (who is assumed to have taken notice of the threat) to assign to the threat body B coming into effect if it is challenged, i.e. if C happens to be the case.*

Definition 4.2.4. *The target credibility, $P_T(C, B)$, of a threat is the subjective conditional probability that the target (promisee) assigns to body B coming into effect if it is challenged (upon having received the threat), i.e. if C happens to be the case.*

Definition 4.2.5. *The threat credibility ratio (TCR, for a positive conditional threat) is defined by the following fraction:*

$$\frac{P_T(C, B)}{P_S(C, B)}$$

Definition 4.2.6. *The intended threat credibility ratio (TCRi, for a positive conditional threat) is defined by the following fraction:*

$$\frac{P_T^i(C, B)}{P_S(C, B)}$$

If the threat credibility ratio (TCR) is high then the target agent is not ignoring the threat and may even overreact on it. If the TCR is low (much lower than 1) then the target agent is likely to fail to take the threat seriously. The idea of TCRi is that it can be assessed by the source without requiring access to any information about the target..

I will model trust of promisee in promiser as a number in the interval $[0, 1]$. Let t be the current trust of T in S. I assume that t is known to target agent T but not to source agent S. Similarly the target credibility of a threat will be known to the target agent but not to the source agent.

4.2.2 THREAT CREDIBILITY DYNAMICS

I propose that the following model for dealing with a sequence of threats from the same source to the same target is used:[39]

1. initially T sets $t = \frac{1}{2}$,

2. if a threat n is received then the target credibility is set equal to t,

3. if a threat m which has previously been received is not kept (that is C is noticed to hold while B is not put into effect) then t is replaced by $\frac{1}{2}t$,

4. if a threat m which has previously been received is challenged and kept (that is C is noticed to hold and subsequently B is indeed put into effect) then t is replaced by $t + \frac{1}{2}(1 - t)$.

This model is transparant for both sides. By producing a sequence of threats and keeping a certain fraction of those, the source agent can make sure that the target agent learns an appropriate level of trust. Then by inspecting its own source credibility for a new threat, the source agent can determine the value of the threat credibility ratio. If that value is low (far below one), then this state of affairs suggests that there is a significant risk of the new threat not being taken sufficiently seriously.

4.3   TOWARDS A HIGH THREAT CREDIBILITY RATIO

Now suppose that putting threat body B into effect is very expensive for S then after making the threat n, S prefers to assign a low source credibility to its threat while at the same time target agent T will assign a high target credibility to the same threat so that a high threat credibility ratio is achieved.

Obtaining a high target credibility can only be achieved by providing a sequences of threats and a history of keeping these threats after being challenged. Doing so may require the use of military force in order to demonstrate that a threat is kept, though with a lower relative cost for the source the cost assessment (by A) for putting body B into effect.

However, using diplomacy alone for the interaction between source agent and target agent it may not be possible to elevate the trust of the target to a sufficiently high level as to make conditional threats sufficiently credible to the target.

Proposition 4.3.1. *By making use of diplomatic means only it is not plausible that one agent (acting as a source agent) can produce a high level of trust in itself by another agent (acting as a target) in such a manner that when the source agent issues a threat towards the target agent with a body involving a high level of aggression, and upon being put into effect coming at a high cost for the source, the threat credibility ratio of that particular threat will be high.*

The implication of this proposition is significant: if state A intends to make use of military superiority over state P, including its nuclear-weapons related superiority over state P, then it must be able to achieve a high TCR for its most dangerous (for the target agent) and costly (for itself upon putting into effect) threats. Creating a high TCR requires that successively several threats are issued, challenged and subsequently kept. Such preliminary threats may need to involve military action rather than diplomatic action.

In other words: if a state A intends to make a state P change its behaviour, and if A is willing to issue threats which, when challenged and kept, require the massive use of military force involving a risk of high military and civilian casualties for A (and perhaps also for Q), then it is rational for A to look for options to issue preparatory threats, the keeping of which may include military actions, which will be challenged and then to keep these threats. Such steps are likely to deviate from a purely diplomatic route.

Proposition 4.3.2. *Politicians who suggest that the US must make use of diplomatic methods only unless and until it is effectively under attack from the DPRK, thereby acknowledge that the US must not and cannot try to reverse the proliferation of nuclear weapons to the DPRK without accepting a fixed and significant risk of serious damage.*

Proposition 4.3.3. *Politicians as referred to in Proposition 4.3.2 hold in low esteem the potential of achieving in a stepwise fashion a high threat credibility ratio against the DPRK in preparation of issuing one or more forceful conditional threats intended to make the opponent reverse.*

4.3.1 CORRECTIONS ON THE DYNAMIC MODEL

The dynamic model for threat credibility ratio evolution as mentioned in this Chapter ignores several factors for which one may seek correction:

Dealing with old threats.
Suppose that there is a package of conditional threats (each with the same source

and target) which are still outstanding, that is which have not been challenged and thereafter either been kept or clearly not kept. Then each of the target credibilities of other outstanding threats is updated in the same manner whenever one of these threats is challenged and depending on it being kept or not kept. This rule merely adds more precision to the description of the dynamics of target threat credibility.

Retrospective threat withdrawal.

Threat withdrawal (also termed threat revocation) may be retrospective, which means that the source now thinks that right from the beginning of a trace of exchanges of promises and threats a certain threat should not have been issued.

In this case the credibilities of outstanding threats may have been influenced by an event of being challenged but not being kept of the threat which is now withdrawn. As a side effect of retrospective threat revocation the dynamics of threat credibilities must be recomputed as if the revoked threat had not been in existence.

Threat withdrawal as a policy change.

Threat withdrawal may constitute a policy change, in which case the past existence of the threat may have made contribution to the evaluation of target credibilities for the other outstanding threats which must not be undone.

Threat overriding.

A threat issued by source sometimes replaces an outstanding threat. There are two cases:

Threat strengthening.

The new threat is stronger than the mentioned outstanding threat. This in turn hay happen in two different ways:

Body extension.

The new threat is equipped with a more comprehensive body so that it is a more serious threat in terms of impact when kept.

Condition weakening.

The new threat has a less comprehensive condition (i.e. weaker condition).

In both cases the new threat replaces the outstanding threat with its source and target credibility unchanged.[40]

Threat weakening.

The new threat is weaker than the outstanding threat: its body is less comprehensive or the condition imposes stronger requirements. The issuing of a weaker threat may be understood as the admission of an error by its source and now it is plausible for both sides to recompute their history of the threat exchange as if the new threat had been in place all the time. Perhaps there will be fewer cases of the source not keeping the new threat so that the target credibility of all outstanding threats (from the same source) increases and the threat credibility ratios increase as well.

Irrationality.

If the leadership of a state panics or otherwise loses track of rational thinking, or if observations regarding the facts on the ground are flawed, it may be the case that a positive conditional threat is kept (that is its body is brought to expression) even if the condition is not satisfied or it may be the case that a negative conditional threat is kept even if the negative condition was satisfied in time. From the viewpoint of the target agent this would be irrational, but following Powell 1985 [46] precisely this type of mechanism must not be ignored. Instead it must be taken into account and it may in fact be constructively used.

Hesitation on moral grounds.

Once a flow of events has taken off in which one or both sides are demonstrating willingness and ability to keep threats they will show no sign of moral hesitation and it is implausible for either side to expect the other side to be stopped, that is to entertain a low source credibility on ethical grounds.

Now it may be the case that unknown to its opponent a side, say A, in the conflict thinks in terms of a red line which it intends not to cross itself although side A is willing to issue conditional threats which when challenged and kept would constitute the crossing of that very red line. This mechanism may lead to a high threat credibility ratio, which may be useful for the source but the same mechanism increases the risk of an overreaction by the target in a later stage.

However, in some case undisclosed moral bounds (privately maintained red lines) may lead to a discount of source credibility, say with a factor 2. It is important for the source to keep in mind that the target won't be able to take this discount into account by sheer lack of information.

Fear of retaliation.

Suppose that source S issues a threat p_s with body B_s under condition C_s to target T. Suppose that T has previously issued a threat p_t with body B_t under the condition C_t to S and that as soon as S puts B_s into effect the condition C_s becomes true so that threat p_s is challenged. Then S must fear retaliation with B_t if it puts B_s into effect. The effect of fear of retaliation is similar to hesitation on moral grounds, T may be hiding its fear for S, and it may also lead to discount of source credibility (for threat p_s) which is undisclosed to the promisee.

These considerations suggest the following conclusion.

Proposition 4.3.4. *Continuous determination of the source credibility of the outstanding threats issued by a source is harder (for the source) than it is to determine the corresponding target credibilities by the target.*

Indeed both the effect of moral hesitation and the effect of fear for retaliation don't allow simplistic quantitative modelling for the source, while both effects may reasonably be ignored by the target.

The source may be weakened by long and difficult internal debating on the how to take morality and fear into account, when working out its own source credibilities. Here lies some possible advice emerging from this work: each side should not underestimate the need to maintain a quantitative perspective on the source credibility, as well as the intended target credibility, an the observed target credibility (in as far as such observations are possible) of its own threats in each stage of the political process. It is unconvincing to perceive a lack of clarity about the credibility of threats primarily at the side of the opponent.

4.4   THREAT EFFECTIVENESS

Effectiveness of a threat is only assessed from the perspective of its source. It is hardly possible to provide a sharp definition of threat effectiveness. In this section I will first discuss credibility and effectiveness.

Definition 4.4.1. *(Tentative definition of threat effectiveness.) A threat is effective if it turns out to be helpful for the source for achieving their objectives.*

I assume that it is important for the source that a source credible threat is also effective. However, both source credible and non-source credible threats may be effective. Here are some cases of threats arguably being effective or ineffective. These should not be read as sharp definitions of notions or types of assessments but merely as illustrations of how assessments of credibility might work in relation to effectiveness.

- *Preparation by warning.* An unconditional source credible threat is effective if upon having been issued by the source it makes the target of the threat respond in a rational manner upon the course of events or the state of affairs upon the threat being kept by its source. That is the threat prepares, as a warning, the target for the event of the threat being kept.[41]

- *Unintended credibility gap.* A source credible unconditional threat may fail to be effective because the target credibility turns out to be unexpectedly low (for the source). As a consequence the target may for instance overreact once the threat is actually kept.

  In this case there is a credibility gap. As a consequence of the credibility gap the target's behaviour may not be impacted by the threat.

- *Intended credibility gap at non-deception.* A source credible threat which has been issued in such a manner as to fail to achieve target credibility, is effective if it increases the effect of surprise for the target upon the threat being kept (counter to target expectation).

- *Credibility gap at deception.* A non-source credible unconditional threat which is nevertheless target credible is effective if it induces costly but irrelevant precautions from the side of the target.

- *Induced target behaviour.* A negative conditional threat is effective if it triggers (causes) the target to act in compliance with the requirements given by the conditions in such a manner as to avoid the threat (body) being put into effect.

- *Failure to induce realistic contemplation of target behaviour.* A source credible threat which for some reason happens not to be target credible upon its reception and which therefore is ignored by the target is non-effective if the target would in hindsight (after the threat has been kept) have preferred to have complied with the requirements of the conditional threat.

- *Induced realistic contemplation of target behaviour.* A source credible conditional threat which turned out to be target credible as well but which fails to achieve adapted target behaviour may still be considered effective (by its source) if the target has made a realistic contemplation of the various aspects of the matter and has taken the likelihood of the threat being kept upon being challenged in due consideration.[42]

4.5   ELEMENTS OF A META-LANGUAGE FOR THREATS

The notion of a threat is far from obvious, and it deviates significantly from the notion of a promise. I hope the following remarks provide further clarification and detail.

Underlying promise.

Each threat is a promise at the same time. I will refer to the promise constituting a threat as its underlying promise. Similarly an implicit threat is an implicit promise at the same time, which is referred to as the underlying implicit promise, and a structural threat is a structural promise at the same time, which is referred to as its underlying structural promise.

Primary and secondary assessment.
Threats differ from promises by requiring a primary assessment made by the promisee (of the negative value of an a outcome of keeping the threat for the promisee) in advance of the threat being kept, and a secondary assessment also made by the promisee that the primary assessment is likely to be shared by a majority of the agents in the scope of the promise (including the promiser).

Target specificity of threats.
For threats the asymmetry between promiser and promisee is more pronounced than for promises which are not considered threats. A promise without a target, i.e. a promise to all agents in scope is conceptually unproblematic, whereas a threat without a target makes little sense. A threat must have been assessed, which can only be done from a particular perspective. Indeed many threats are unlikely to be detrimental (upon effectuation) for the promiser.

Promising to accept a threat.
Misunderstandings are possible if a promise which was meant by the promiser to be understood as a threat is not viewed as a threat, and conversely. In order to avoid misunderstandings, the promisee of a threat can accept the threat by notifying (promising) the promiser that it has taken notice of the promise and that it has taken it for a threat.[43]

Typing of threats: inference based in the form of a negative condition.
While it is common to say "I promise you X provided C comes about" it is quite uncommon to say for instance: "I threaten you (with) X provided C comes about". This is a matter of language conventions. Explicit typing of a promise (by referring to it as a promise during delivery) by the promiser is far more common than explicit typing of a threat as such by the promiser (source) of its underlying promise. When receiving a conditional promise an agent in scope must often infer from the form whether it is meant as a threat, and in particular the form of the condition will play a role. If C read " you made a payment of an amount a (in a certain manner as indicated) before the deadline d expires" the promise clearly serves as a threat.[44]

Typing of threats: flagging the underlying promise as a warning.
While the utterance "I promise you, if you do X then I will do Y" is a common

way to express a promise, the corresponding threat is more commonly phrased as a warning: "I warn you, if you do X then I will do Y".

Primary and secondary assessment taken for granted.

The promise "I promise you X unless C comes about" may well qualify as a threat in spite of the explicit typing as a promise. This is the case if it is taken for granted that the primary and secondary assessment of the value to the target of X being put into effect have a satisfactory outcome, that is an outcome consistent with the promise being classiofied as a threat.

4.6   Meta-threats, explicit threats, and implicit threats

A meta-threat is a threat about a promise or threat. In other words, a meta-threat is a meta-promise which at the same time qualifies as a threat. For instance the meta-promise "I promise you "that A will promise you to go to war with your country" if you don't give in to A's requests within a week" qualifies as a threat, and for that reason is a meta-threat. Meta-threats are quite relevant as a A threat is plausibly reported by some messenger by means of a meta-promise which plausibly qualifies as a meta-threat.

4.6.1   Explicit threats versus implicit threats

An explicit threat is an explicit promise which is a threat according to the criteria mentioned in the beginning of Section 4. An implicit threat is a threat which, without being issued by its source as an utterance, is nevertheless present and the existence of which can be plausibly guessed or inferred by an agent. For instance the presence of dogs behind a fence constitutes an implicit promise (with any potential trespasser as a promisee, and all bypassing persons in scope), qualifying as a threat, of problems to be expected when trespassing without proper admission. A sign "beware of the dogs" turns the implicit threat into an explicit one. Even in the absence of dogs the sign is an implicit threat, though in that case the threat is a deception.

An agent who discovers an implicit threat will usually convey the implicit threat as the body of a meta-promise. For instance: "I promise you that, "according to the owner's (implicit) threat to all potential illegal trespassers, when trespassing without authorisation, you are likely to be hurt by the dogs protecting the area and you cannot complain about having been hurt afterwards because you have been properly warned in advance of entering the area, although this warning has not been made very explicit".

4.6.2 ALLEGED IMPLICIT THREATS

An alleged threat is comparable to an implicit threat with the difference that the source of the threat may not have intended any of its behaviour or utterances to be recognised as a threat by the target or by agents in scope. An alleged threat is said (promised) to exist by an observer who forwards it to an audience thereby providing itself target and scope. Alleged threats may result from mistaken copying of explicit threats or from mistaken recognition of implicit threats. An alleged threat may be an implicit threat if the allegation turns out to be valid.

If "A promises B to do "body" unless "condition" is fulfilled, with scope S" then P may communicate the unconditional version of the threat instead:

> P promises to Q with scope S (including A and B) that "A has promised B
> to do "body", with scope S"

Now P's promise communicates an alleged threat rather than an actual threat, because it is not guaranteed, and not plausible that A meant to issue an unconditional threat.

4.7 STRUCTURAL THREATS

A structural threat is a state of affairs which can be recognised, though not routinely, as a potential implicit threat. A structural threat is discovered rather than issued.[45]

A structural threat is comparable to an alleged threat but without having a source. A structural threat is plausibly communicated by means of a meta-promise, which in may well constitute a meta-threat. A structural threat is complementary to a structural promise in terms of assessment of the value of implications of its being kept for the target. Structural threats may or may not have conditions.

A structural threat in the case of the KCW is: "the DPRK is successfully developing miniaturisation of its nuclear bombs, both fission bombs and fusion bombs, and is likely to be able to mount nuclear weapons on an IRBM and on an ICBM within 5 years."

An example of a conditional structural threat (with target B) is: "if the agricultural use of antibiotics remains at the current levels then in 2030 the occurrence of resistent bacteria will be so common that this puts your (B's) entire family at risk".

4.8 A HIERARCHY OF LEVELS OF ABSTRACTION FOR PROMISES AND THREATS

As stated above different notions of promise and threat correspond to different collections of features that are assumed to be present in excess of the ground features. However, an even mored rudimentary form of classification is needed for promises and threats. The following levels of abstraction are useful:

Naming level.
> A mere name may refer to a promise or threat if it is sufficiently well-known. For instance, the "threat of war" may have a common meaning for an entire population of one or more nations during some episode.

Outline level.
> An outline level threat consists of a brief description of it. For instance: the threat by state A that it will destroy a specific nuclear power plant in state P by means of a missile attack. An outline description of a promise or threat includes a naming level description.

Ground level.
> A promise or threat is specified in terms of its ground features.

Refined level with features from feature set W.
> Each subset W of the collection of features constitutes a refined level. A promise or threat is specified at level W if the features of W have been detailed.

Refined level.
> A promise or threat is specified at a refined level if for some W. In practice W can be read off from the specification, rather than that it has been detailed in advance of the presentation of a promise or threat.

4.8.1   PROMISE–THREAT BUNDLES

When describing a status quo including the positions of various states it is useful to specify combinations of promises and threats that have been issued by the parties involved. In practice promise–threat bundles, if collected at all, will consist of promises and threats specified at different levels of abstraction, and may involve implicit as wel as structural promises and threats.

4.9   RISKS AND LIES

Closely related to the concept of threat is the concept of risk. Somewhat related is the notion of a lie. I will discuss risk and lies in this Section. Obviously at a naming level promises, threats, risks, and lies cannot be distinguished.

At the outline level making distinctions is difficult too. For instance the threat of a specific attack, the risk of that attack, the existence of a risk of that attack, the assertion that a risk of that atack exists, are hard to distinguish, and "the existence of a risk of a certain attack" might be also considered a deception or a lie. the assertion.

It lies beyond the scope of this work to develop a detailed account of risk, lie, and deception and to establish convincing connections with Promise Theory and its extension with threats. Some remarks about the relative status of these concepts are in order.

4.10 RISK VERSUS THREAT

A risk, once discovered, is a the unconditional form of a structural threat. A risk has a target, the agent or agents that are at risk. An unrevealed risk is a potential structural threat. A risk may be discovered by some agents and at the same time be undiscovered by other agents. When a risk (viewed as embedded in a promise) is kept I will speak of the occurrence of a risk event (for the risk at hand).

Discovering risks is done in a process called risk analysis. The following proposition encodes an attempt to specify the relation between risk and threat.[46]

Proposition 4.10.1. *A known risk for target T is the body of a known structural conditional threat (in some cases the body of a known implicit or of an explicit threat which has been issued, and in case of an alleged threat the risk will be an alleged risk) aimed at target T, which has both a low probability of being challenged and a low probability of being kept conditional upon being challenged.*

From this proposition it follows that one need not, and in fact cannot assign a probability to a risk unless the probability of the condition being challenged is taken into account as well.

4.10.1 EXAMPLES OF RISKS I: FLIGHT INCIDENTS

The risk of becoming victim a of a plane crash can only be quantified upon assigning a probability to the condition of flying. Quantifying the risk of a plane crash requires its embedding in a structural threat and in particular that requires a choice of a target. Quite different targets can be imagined. The probability of risk event occurrence for a person on the ground differs for the risk of a passenger, and differs from the risks incurred by the owners or operators of the plane or the risks for fire fighters and members of rescue teams. In each case the specific risk being dependant on their respective roles.

4.10.2 EXAMPLES OF RISKS II: KILLER ROBOTS GROWING UP

As another example consider so-called killer robots. These may be proposed as a promise within the coming to an audience which may be inclined and able to make use of such weapons, the same promise may be understood as a threat by a state that is unable or unwilling to acquire the use of such weapons. A hostile state H (from the perspective of a state A) being able to acquire killer robots in significant numbers within 5 years may be understood as a threat while the scenario that H will actually use its killer robots against A is estimated so low that the latter (i.e. the actual use of killer robots by P after having become available to P) merely counts as a risk rather than as a threat.

4.11   LIE VERSUS PROMISE

If A promises to B that A has made a transfer of an amount a of money to B, then this utterance may qualify as a lie, at least when taking the first definition of a lie in Mahon 2016 [39] as a criterion for lying. The complexity of the notion of a lie appears from the long list of alternative definitions of a lie which has been compiled by Mahon. Specifying the relation between promises and lies in more detail, however, requires that neighbouring notions like fact, alternative fact, news, fake news, deception, and opinion are taken as well into account. These considerations have not yet been detailed in a satisfactory manner in the context of Promise Theory.

Here is an attempt to incorporate the notion of a lie in Promise Theory while still leaving freedom for the choice of a definition of lying. In the case of a lie the promiser is referred to as a liar and I propose the promisee to be referred to as its target.

Proposition 4.11.1. *A lie is a special case of a factual promise. The body of a lie contains an assertion which is false in the eyes of the promiser (the liar). A lie is a special case of a deceitful promise. A lie is a promise of fake fact.*

This Proposition is quite sensitive to one's preferred definition of a lie. In fact it fails to convey the idea (as required in first definition of a lie in Mahon 2016 [39]) that the liar (the promiser of the promise under scrutiny of being a lie) intends to make the promisee think in agreement with the body of the promise. In the context of promises it is conceivable that a lie is not intended to make the target think in conformance with the body of the lie, but to convince the target that none of the agents in scope of the lie are willing to stand up and to confront the liar with the falsity of its promise.

Chapter 5

Alternative facts and alternative histories

The fact that both sides in the Korean Cold War disagree on which side initiated the military conflict may seem odd but such discrepancies may be the rule rather than the exception with the commencement of a war. The accounts on the first exchanges on WW II in Poland and on the start of the war in Vietnam were divergent and so are recent accounts on the war in the Eastern part of Ukraine. Promise Theory is flexible in that it requires a low commitment to any notion or concept of truth, whereas it attributes a more prominent role to the concept of trust, while allowing a promiser to be trusted differently by different agents in their audience.

If one is handed over food in a restaurant, the fact of edibility of the particular specimen is conveyed by way of an implicit promise of edibility which the customer receives and understands from a background of trust, or in rare cases lack of trust. The truth of the assertion that the specimen was safely edible, however defined, is usually left unanalysed unless, unfortunately, it turned out not to have been safely edible.

5.1 Disclaimer

I shall not claim that Promise Theory can do away with an notion of truth in a philosophical sense as if a useful version of analytical philosophy may be built merely on the notion of a promise. Promise Theory is not committed to a denial of the existence of facts but Promise Theory contemplates the world, by way of a thought experiment, as if all facts are promises while paying less attention to the idea that some promises of fact constitute "true" facts.

Recent political developments in the US have brought to prominence the phrase "alternative fact". Alternative facts may be stated as if factual information is provided while at the same time alternative facts are (intentionally) unrelated to any empirical or scientific support. In spite of these deficiencies alternative facts may be highly influential. Accepting alternative facts as somehow in the same league as facts is compatible with the assumption that "fact" is merely another word for promise, at least in a political context. Alternative facts are promise-like because these critically relate to trust in the producer of such utterances, just as promises do. By speaking of alternative facts it is highlighted at the same time that so-called facts are promise-like.

Proposition 5.1.1. *Facts and alternative facts share the disposition of being usefully cast as promises. Once understood as promises facts and alternative facts become hard to distinguish.*

Proposition 5.1.2. *Once a fact has been stated or written by a source, each agent in its audience unavoidably converts it to the status of a factual promise which has been issued by that same source.*

Proposition 5.1.3. *Truth of a fact (viewed as a promise) is merely a degree of consensus about it among the agents in its scope. The coming about of consensus is primarily a matter of free will of agents, who may be ignorant, or even deliberately ignorant, of scientific or other evidence. Power may drive the coming about of some form of consensus. In other words: truth of a factual promise is a matter of power.*

Proposition 5.1.4. *Political facts, including political alternative facts, are plausibly viewed as promises.*

This work is written under the (hopefully simplifying) assumption that there are no political or historical facts, just political and historical promises.

5.2   ALTERNATIVE FACTS AND THE STRENGTHENING OF TRUST

If a politician P claims (promises) that say measles is not an infectuous disease (s)he may very well know that this is not true, and that agents in P's audience will acquire an increased trust upon making their own assessment that measles is not infectuous. Still by producing this alternative fact P may strengthen the trust of agents in scope because of the very ability of P deal in political terms with the negative response which may be expected upon issuing such an utterance.

5.3 ACTIONABLE PROMISES, FACTUAL PROMISES, AND FACTS

If agent A asserts a description of fact f to agent B then, according to Promise Theory this event counts as issuing a promise irrespective of f being true. Indeed, whether or not B accepts f, or updates and upgrades its subjective probability assignment to f, will primarily depend on B's trust in A.[47] Moreover if at some stage B must conclude that A told a lie (an alternative fact in recent jargon), a side-effect is likely to be a downgrading of A's trust in B. Agents are likely to take facts (i.e. assertions of characteristics of the state of affairs) for granted on the basis of trust, rather than on the basis of recognition of truth.

When discussing communication between human agents it seems to be less plausible to label each exchange of information as a promise. The use of promises is facilitated by speaking of a factual promise if a promise transfers information (whether true or not) and speaking of an actionable promise if in addition the promiser predicts, either explicitly or implicitly, a role of its own in the process of keeping the promise.

Nevertheless, any speaker or author may wish to base their exposition on a catalogue of facts which are, even if cast as factual promises, assumed to be true as working assumptions. Casting such assumptions as promises is unhelpful, and casting these as "assertions of fact" leaves the task to the public to cast these assertions as promises issued by the author as a source with the members of the audience as the promisee(s), and to make up their mind on matters of truth.

Proposition 5.3.1. *In a political (or otherwise non-technical) exposition an author will state facts by way of assumptions, thereby deliberately ignoring that, as viewed from the perspective of a reader,[48] these facts merely have the status of promises issued by the author.*

Promises of fact may be attributed with a subjective probability, expressing the probability (of truth) of the fact in the eyes of its author. Promises of fact are formulated in such a manner that the probability is at least 50%. Otherwise the negation of the body may be taken as a body for a complementary promise which satisfies that criterion.

Proposition 5.3.2. *When stating facts which serve as assumptions for an exposition it is reasonable to provide subjective probabilities as an indication of the level of certainty of the source (of the facts viewed as promises). For a fact the probability always exceeds 50%, otherwise only its negation may be stated as a fact.*

The distinction between facts and questions is merely a matter of subjective probability. Whence the following definition.

Definition 5.3.1. *A factual question is a fact*[49] *with a subjective (source) probability below 75%.*

5.4 PROMISE THEORY IN A WORLD OF ALTERNATIVE FACTS

In a world where alternative facts are spread via various media just as efficiently as are "true" facts, Promise Theory may provide a meta-theory by focusing attention on the major role of the concept of trust. From the point of view of Promise Theory the situation is simple: if an agent X issues a factual promise p that is demonstrably wrong, and the agents in scope of the promise don't decrease their trust in X then all of this proves that the agents in scope have a very high trust in X. The dynamics of trust, however, is a difficult theme, and simply expecting an agent to demolish their trust base in a parliamentary democracy by repeatedly issuing mistaken factual promises is unwarranted. By issuing factual promises which are being revealed as fake rather than true political agents do not erode their trust base as quickly as many observers might have hoped or believed.

Promise Theory provides no clue on how the updating of trust on the basis of promise assessment by promisees and other agents in scope of a promise actually works. That mechanism, or rather its outcome, is a parameter for Promise Theory and not something which it pretends to explain.

5.5 THE IMPORTANCE OF ALTERNATIVE HISTORY

A generalisation to history of the idea that facts are promises rather than the other way around, thereby putting facts and alternative facts in the same basket, is to accept that only alternative histories exist.

Historical research may consist of the production of an alternative history which suits one's objectives. Promise Theory does not advocate the end of history as a social science with a solid methodology enabling it to arrive at unambiguous results in the long run, but Promise Theory suggest to contemplate a political issue in a simplified manner as if only alternative histories exist. An alternative history, in its capacity of representing the views of a side in a conflict, may be encoded as a collection of promises which have been made by that side during a relevant time frame.

Of course a meticulous study of history, with a focus on the discovery of true and stable facts which can be accepted by all sides involved, may be helpful to understand current events, even more so than a contemplation of alternative history might be. But the impact of a particular brand of alternative history may be very significant, and escaping from the influence of a specific alternative history that dominates the discourse in a state or community which is engaged in a serious conflict may be impossible in the given time frame, in particular when the conflict is hot. For that reason an open minded scrutiny of alternative history (or histories) may be helpful in order to create practical perspectives as well as operational options.

Finding a unified and uncontroversial description of Korean history is difficult. Breuker 2012 [16] states:

> We need to know why hundreds of millions are spent in China and South Korea to determine whose version of North Korean and North Chinese ancient history is right. We have to understand how important the historical narratives of Kim Il Sung's day as a Manchurian guerrilla still are. We also need to know how different perceptions of what happened brought us to this place and how these are aiding or obstructing possible solutions.

Different perceptions of history (different alternative histories) serve as motivating factors for different sides in the KCW. Although historical research may settle such differences on the long run, it probably won't achieve that form of scholarly conflict resolution on a time scale needed to support either side in the current conflict.

Proposition 5.5.1. *Political histories, including political alternative histories are plausibly viewed as bundles of factual promises.*

5.6 SCIENTIFIC FACTS, LEGAL FACTS, AND POLITICAL FACTS

One may distinguish facts as scientific, legal (and juridical), and political. For each of these categories a balance between established fact and promise of fact can be made. Relevant to the topics discussed in this monograph is the following Proposition.

Proposition 5.6.1. *The status of political facts is itself a political matter.*

(i) There is no guaranteed or smooth transfer from scientific fact to political fact. In other words: scientific fact is entitled, merely on the basis of the rigour and and methodology of the scientific process, to the status of an undisputed political fact.

(ii) There is no guaranteed or smooth transfer from legal fact to political fact.

5.7   THE EARTH MAY BE FLAT, AT LEAST AS A POLITICAL FACT!

Taking Proposition 5.6.1 to the extreme, an important conclusion is obtained: there is nothing wrong in principle with a politician who proposes that the earth is flat in spite of overwhelming scientific evidence to the contrary. An uniformed supporter base may subscribe to this unorthodox view and may validate it during elections or in popularity polls as a live political fact at least for some time.

Political facts are always subject to the political process. No political fact established in some episode is immune against being denied in a subsequent episode. The pipeline from the scientific process and the legal process to fact finding in the political process requires a constant attention and scrutiny from all citizens who appreciate compliance between these categories.

CHAPTER 6

DETERRENCE UNDER SYMMETRIC CONDITIONS

I will work in the neorealist paradigm as explained in Waltz 1990 [67] by paying attention to the compositional structure of a two or more interacting units (states) and by trying to focus on types of interaction and structure rather than on bottom up explanation of observed phenomena and events, with a focus on the internal structure and working of states.

Rather than speaking of actual states I will speak of A, B, C, P, Q, R. Although generality is meant at the same time I will have the following interpretation of these abstract names in mind: A = US, B = ROK, C = Japan, P = DPRK, Q = PRC, R = Russia. It will easily be understood from the context

if this specific interpretation is meant for A, B, C, P, Q, and R, rather than a general one.

I will first provide a listing of outline level promise descriptions that may be exchanged between nuclear-weapons states. This listing serves the purpose of introducing relevant terminology in a setting of Promise Theory.

Thereafter I wil provide a survey of some refined level descriptions of promises and threats which may be unilaterally issued by one state towards another state.

6.1   A SURVEY OF RELEVANT OUTLINE LEVEL PROMISES

I will now specify some promises between nuclear-weapons states A and P, each of which have the whole world as scope. There promises are specified in outline level (see

Section 4.8).

successful counterforce strike capability promise:

A promises P that it is (considers itself to be) able to perform a first strike which prevents P from performing a second strike.

successful surgical counterforce strike capability promise:

A promises P that it is able to perform a surgical first strike which prevents P from performing a second strike.

A surgical strike protects civilian life (except for mistakes which wil be limited in number and seriousness) and focuses exclusively on military targets.

successful conventional counterforce strike capability promise:

A promises P that it is able to perform a first strike making use of conventional weapons only which prevents P from performing a second strike.

successful conventional surgical counterforce strike capability promise:

A promises P that it is able to perform a surgical first strike making use of conventional weapons only which prevents B from performing a second strike.

first strike capability promise:

A promises B that it is able to perform a first strike which is highly detrimental for B (though it may not prevent P from performing a second strike, that is the first strake may not be a counterforce strike as well).

conventional first strike capability promise:

A promises P that it is able to perform a conventional first strike which is highly detrimental for B (though it may not prevent P from performing a second strike).

anticipated first strike capability promise:

A promises P that it will able within a limited amount of time (say k months) to perform a first strike which is highly detrimental for P (though it may not prevent P from performing a second strike).

The time frame of k months or less may be needed either for development and production of nuclear weapons, or for the miniaturisation thereof, or for the development and production of delivery technology by way IRBM, ICBM, cruise missile or otherwise.

immediate full second strike promise:

A promises P that upon a first strike (either a devastating attack or a serious attempt to perform a first counterforce strike, whether surgical or not) by P, A can and will retaliate with a full (that is devastating, that is likely to come with many civilian casualties) second strike on P, and that P will do so without further delay or deliberation.

This promise is equivalent to the promise from A to P that it holds that P cannot perform a successful counterforce strike on A.

immediate full and conventional second strike promise:

A promises P that upon an devastating attack (first strike) by P, A can and will retaliate with a conventional but devastating second strike on P, and that P will do so without delay.

This promise is unlikely to be kept as conventional forces are quite vulnerable to conventional attacks, but it is not impossible that A can keep this promise.

delayed full second strike promise:

A promises P that upon and after completion of an devastating attack (first strike) by P on A, A certainly can and probably (with a subjective probability of 75%) will retaliate with a second strike on P, though P will do so only with some delay and after due consideration of the facts on the ground and in the light of what is considered to be in the best interests of A.

delayed full and conventional second strike promise:

A promises a delayed full second strike and in addition A promises that its second strike will be carried out by means of conventional weapons only.

mutually assured destruction:

the combination (conjunction) of the full second strike promise from A to P and the full second strike promise from P to A.

disproportional second strike promise:

A promises P that it is able (and intends to) to perform a full second strike after even a moderate and conventional attack by P on A has taken place.

general non-nuclear strike promise:

A promises to all states that it will never be the first user of nuclear weapons in a conflict.

limited non-nuclear strike promise:

A promises to each non-nuclear-weapons states that it will never be the first user of nuclear weapons in a conflict with that state.

symmetric non-nuclear strike promise:

A promises to P (a nuclear-weapons state) that it will react to a non-nuclear attack by means of non-nuclear counter measures only.

counterforce only nuclear strike promise:
> A promises B that it will not use nuclear weapons against civilian targets.

recognition as a nuclear-weapons state:
> A promises to recognise P as a nuclear-weapons state, an to recognise its right to develop effective means of delivery for the nuclear weapon in is possession at least towards A.

temporary recognition as a nuclear-weapons state:
> A promises to recognise P as a nuclear-weapons state, though A does not recognise P's right to develop effective means of delivery for the nuclear weapon in is possession at towards A (and possibly towards other states).

rejection of long–term nuclear-weapons state status:
> A promises to work against P as long as it upholds its ambitions to constitute a nuclear-weapons state.

conditional non-recognition of the nuclear-weapons status:
> As long as A and P are in a state of war (notwithstanding the presence of an armistice) A upholds the promise of rejecting P's long term nuclear-weapons state status.

6.2   UNILATERAL NUCLEAR DETERRENCE

I will assume that a state A may claim to deter another state B from engaging in a action, say X, without B actually being deterred by A from doing X. Indeed A will never know for sure that B is deterred from doing X until B, by doing X, demonstrates that deterrence does not apply or has applied in some phase but has ended. And if that happens, i.e. B performs X, then A may not be able to find out if, before that action, B's not doing X was caused by B being deterred by A from doing so, or by some other cause.

By issuing a promise and a threat A may reach the military–political status quo of unilateral nuclear deterrence towards B. As an optional aspect A may promise future proof reliable means of weapon delivery to B.

promise

name claim of adequate nuclear strike capability towards B.

source government of A

body availing of and ability and intention to maintain a nuclear strike
capability in the direction of B, consisting of these 7 components:

Nuclear weapons in stock. A maintains a significant (sufficient, but possibly undisclosed) number of nuclear weapons of various sizes and kinds (A-weapon, N-weapon, or H-weapon, tactical or strategic).

Reliable means of weapon delivery. A has (at the time of issuing and assuming that B's defensive capabilities against nuclear are left unchanged) the ability to successfully deliver (and bring to explosion) nuclear weapons over all relevant targets inside the mainland of B.

(Optional) future proof reliable means of weapon delivery. A will keeps the ability to successfully deliver (and bring to explosion) nuclear weapons over all relevant targets inside the mainland of B as long as B develops its defensive systems, in agreement with the promises it has made.

Construction ability. A maintains the capability, involving research, development and production, to develop and build nuclear weapons and delivery systems.

Technology up to date. A maintains for its nuclear forces a level of technology which allows use at will, prevents spurious use, and does not allow B to protect its mainland or forces from being attacked with nuclear weapons, even if a significant fraction of those may be intercepted in case of an attack.

Second strike capability. A maintains its weapons systems in such a manner that B cannot perform a (first) counterforce strike, either surgical or wholly destructive (for A).

First strike capability. A maintains at any time a first strike capability towards B, which may go far beyond a surgical counterforce strike. In particular, A will maintain military planning for a first strike against B.

Field exercises. A will perform the field exercises needed to maintain the aforementioned capabilities.

target government of B

timespan indefinite.

claim. (Upon the promise having been issued) the military–political status quo includes: A may threaten B with unilateral nuclear deterrence.

scope government and population of B plus UN Security Council.

By combining a version of the adequate nuclear strike capability promise with a version of the threat of nuclear retaliation (see immediately below the following 4 definitions) various forms of claims to nuclear deterrence (of B by A) are obtained.

Definition 6.2.1. *The military–political status quo of* **weak and cautious unilateral deterrence** *of B is reached by A after having issued the above promise of "claim of adequate nuclear strike capability towards B" without "future proof reliable means of delivery" option, as well as having issued the following "threat of nuclear retaliation with no first use guarantee".*

Definition 6.2.2. *The military–political status quo of* **weak unilateral deterrence** *of B, by A is reached by A after having issued the above promise of "claim of adequate nuclear strike capability towards B" without "future proof reliable means of delivery" option, as well as having issued the following "threat of nuclear retaliation without no first use guarantee".*

Definition 6.2.3. *The military–political status quo of* **strong and cautious unilateral deterrence** *of B is reached by A after having issued the above promise of "claim of adequate nuclear strike capability towards B" with "future proof reliable means of delivery" option, as well as having issued the following "threat of nuclear retaliation with no first use guarantee".*

Definition 6.2.4. *The military–political status quo of* **strong unilateral deterrence** *of B, by A is reached by A after having issued the above promise of "claim of adequate nuclear strike capability towards B" with "future proof reliable means of delivery" option, as well as having issued the following "threat of nuclear retaliation without no first use guarantee".*

> **threat**
>
> **name** threat of nuclear retaliation (optionally with no first use guarantee).
>
> **source** government of A
>
> **body** effective retaliation in the direction of B, consisting of these 6 components:
>
>> **retaliation without further warning.** A will retaliate when and where it deems appropriate, with its own methods, and without further advance warning.
>>
>> **operations involving nuclear weapons.** A attacks B (mainland of B as well as forces of B outside its mainland) with operations involving nuclear weapons.

deterrence intended. The attacks are so forceful that no lasting gains are to be expected for B from its initial aggression towards A.

Very significant civilian losses expected. The attacks may lead to civilian casualties and are not limited to a surgical counterforce strike.[50]

No guarantee of proportionality. Because the main objective of the threat is deterrence of B there is no guarantee that A's response will be proportional to the attack of B.

No time bound. There is also no time bound on the duration of A's operations, merely stopping its actions or even offering surrender by B may not suffice to stop A's operations.

target government of B

positive condition The conjunction of two (optionally 3) conditions:

need for military action B attacks A, or otherwise acts in a manner which A cannot possibly accept and endure,

conventional weapons do not suffice. Without the use of nuclear weapons aimed at bringing damage to B, A cannot bring B's aggression to a halt.

(Optional) no first use guarantee. B has already made use of nuclear weapons in the mentioned operations against A.

timespan indefinite.

claim. A maintains unilateral nuclear deterrence towards B.

scope government and population of B plus UN Security Council.

6.3 ARMS RACE AVOIDING UNILATERAL NUCLEAR DETERRENCE

Arms race avoiding unilateral nuclear deterrence involves an additional promise, which aims to allow B to achieve reciprocal nuclear deterrence towards A without forcing B into a costly technological development which may even bring the credibility of A's unilateral nuclear deterrence of B to an end, unless A also engages and succeeds in expensive research, development, production, and deployment of novel offensive weapons systems.

promise

name conditional defensive limitation promise from A to B.[51]

source government of A

body limitation of anti–nuclear-weapons defensive systems, consisting of these 3 components:

> **Parameter** $k_{abm} \in \mathbb{N}$.
>
> **Limiting the number of ABM systems.** A will not deploy more than k_{abm} ABM missiles.
>
> **Limiting the technology underlying ABM systems.** A will limit the intelligence of its ABM systems so that B need not worry about the expected reliability and credibility of its own nuclear-weapon loaded missiles (IRBM's or ICBM's).
>
> **limiting the potential of a surgical first counterforce strike.**

deadline for effectuation upon being challenged. Immediate.[52]

target government of B

positive condition A and B have both signed the "anti–nuclear weapons defensive system limitation agreement".

timespan until either A or B withdraws its (conditional resp. unconditional) limitation promise, or is not kept by the other side, or has become outdated in terms of technology.

claim. A facilitates stable nuclear deterrence of B towards itself.[53]

scope government and population of B plus UN Security Council.

After A has issued the conditional defensive limitation promise towards B, and B has issued the (symmetric) conditional defensive limitation promise towards A, both A and B can simultaneously challenge theses promises by signing the following agreement:

Agreement (anti–nuclear weapons defensive system limitation agreement) hereby A and B (place p, date d) agree that:

(i) A has issued the conditional defensive limitation promise from A to B,

(ii) B has issued the conditional defensive limitation promise from B to A,

(iii) Both A and B intend to avoid an extremely costly and unpredictable technology race for better defensive systems and for better nuclear weapons delivery technology in order to deal with the other side's improved defensive capabilities,and

(iv) A and B promise to one-another that they will allow regular inspections in order to see to it that both defensive limitation promises are kept.

6.4 CLAIMING COUNTERFORCE STRIKE CAPABILITY

Different forms of attack that may involve the use of nuclear weapons must be distinguished.

Definition 6.4.1. *Counterforce strike and counterforce strike capability:*

(i) A counterforce strike by A on B is an attack by A on B which deprives B of the option to launch a strike on A.

(ii) A counterforce strike is surgical if it leads to limited civilian damage and casualties, otherwise it is destructive.

(iii) A has a counterforce strike capability against B at some stage if A is able to launch a counterforce strike against A.

(iv) A has a surgical counterforce strike capability at some stage if A is able to launch a counterforce strike against B.

(v) A has a delayed counterforce strike capability at some stage if A is able to launch a counterforce strike against B in response of any sustained first strike of B.

Promises regarding counterforce strike capability take a different form, for instance:

Promise 6.4.1. *The chief of staff of the forces of A promises the government of A (with selected generals and politicians in scope) that the army of A has a first counterforce strike capability against B.*

Promise 6.4.2. *The chief of staff of the forces of A promises the government of A (with selected generals and politicians in scope) that the armed forces of A have no surgical first counterforce strike capability against B and in addition the armed forces of B have no delayed counterforce strike capability against B.*

Promise 6.4.3. *The chief of staff of the forces of A promises the government of A (with selected generals and politicians in scope) that the army of A has no first or delayed counterforce strike capability against B whatsoever.*

To date information about the presence or absence of counterforce stroke capabilities seems to be classified in all cases. At best the public media provide speculative information on such matters. By lack of any experience and of any experimental evidence politicians must develop their views on the basis of promises that have been made by the commanders of the armed forces.

6.5   FIRST COUNTERFORCE STRIKE CAPABILITY AS A THREAT

Claiming a first counterforce strike capability may be done by issuing the following threat.

> **threat**
>
> **name** claiming first counterforce strike capability in the direction of B.
>
> **source** government of A
>
> **body** the body consists of these 6 components:
>
> > **attack without warning.** A is able to attack when and where it deems appropriate, with its own methods, and without further advance warning.
> >
> > **destroying the enemy's second strike capability.** A first counterforce strike by A on B deprives B from the option to carry out a second strike against A.
> >
> > **operations involving nuclear weapons.** A attacks B (mainland of B as well as forces of B outside its mainland) with operations involving nuclear weapons.
> >
> > **Significant civilian losses expected.** The attacks may lead to civilian casualties and are not limited to a surgical counterforce strike.[54]
> >
> > **(Optional) surgical first strike.** Optionally it may be predicted that a surgical strike is performed which limits the number of civilian casualties to a reasonable minimum.
> >
> > **No time bound.** There is no time bound on the duration of A's operations, merely stopping its actions or even offering surrender by B may not suffice to stop A's operations.
>
> **target** government of B
>
> **positive condition** B has started an attack on A since date d (the date of A's issuing of the promise at hand):
>
> **timespan** indefinite.
>
> **claim.** A maintains unilateral counterforce strike capability towards B.
>
> **scope** government and population of B plus UN Security Council.

6.6 CLAIMING A DELAYED COUNTERFORCE STRIKE CAPABILITY

A much stronger threat consists of a delayed counterforce strike capability. Allowing a delay means that B won't be able to frustrate A's counterforce strike capability by a first strike of its own.

threat

name claiming delayed counterforce strike capability in the direction of B.

source government of A

body the body consists of these 7 components:

attack without warning. A is able to attack when and where it deems appropriate, with its own methods, and without further advance warning. A is able to perform an attack after (and responding to) a first strike on A has already been delivered by B.

destroying the enemy's continued strike capability. A delayed counterforce strike by A on B deprives B from the option to carry out further attacks on A.

operations involving nuclear weapons. A attacks B (mainland of B as well as forces of B outside its mainland) with operations involving nuclear weapons.

deterrence intended. The attacks are so forceful that no lasting gains are to be expected for B from its initial aggression towards A.

Significant civilian losses expected. The attacks may lead to civilian casualties and are not limited to a surgical counterforce strike.

No guarantee of proportionality. Because the main objective of the threat is deterrence of B there is no guarantee that A's response will be proportional to the attack of B.

No time bound. There is also no time bound on the duration of A's operations, merely stopping its actions or even offering surrender by B may not suffice to stop A's operations.

target government of B

positive condition B has not started any attack on A since date d (the date of A's issuing of the promise at hand):

timespan indefinite.

claim. A maintains unilateral counterforce strike capability towards B irrespective of a first strike by B.

scope government and population of B plus UN Security Council.

Chapter 7

An unbiased perspective on the Korean Cold War?

Writing about the KCW as a case study regarding a topic in nuclear deterrence theory one may easily miss the observation that the US versus DPRK antagonism is both important and exceptional for several reasons: (i) is the first occurrence of a major conflict between asymmetrically weaponised nuclear-weapon states, (ii) is as paradigmatic for the subject of nuclear deterrence as the case of the US versus the USSR has been 50 years ago, and (iii) has the status of a defining case rather than of a mere example.

The US versus DPRK antagonism proves that sharply asymmetric conditions governing a cold war between nuclear-weapons states can actually occur, just as the US versus USSR antagonism has demonstrated the reality of fairly symmetric conditions in such a cold war. When positioning the KCW as a paradigmatic case care must be taken not to qualify the same case as some political rarity, say mainly caused by US neglect, or because the DPRK is considered an exceptional case. The case is of exceptional importance and an impartial description of the conflict is needed to capture and solidify its status as a paradigmatic case for decades to come, if not for centuries.

When proposing to view the antagonism of the DPRK and the US as being of a comparable heuristic value for the theory of nuclear deterrence as the antagonism between the USSR and the US has been in the past then some form of a neutral description of the state of affairs must be given. Neutrality is hard to achieve, and judging whether or not it has been achieved is not up to the author. Striving for neutrality may also be considered wrong by those readers who feel that in moral terms one of both sides is without any possible doubt at at a higher ground and that a failure by an author to notice that fact constitutes a proof of a wrong attitude. One can't have it both ways and my

"

plan is to provide a sketch of the positions of both sides of the conflict around 2017 in a manner which is unbiased. That a reasonably unbiased presentation is given amounts to a promise I make to the reader, the assessment of which, of course is left to the reader. I will try to achieve an unbiased perspective by including (potentially) biased views from both sides and by not making any additional assessments myself.

It is the case that both sides disagree on many aspects of their antagonistic relation. I have tried to list some of these aspects, in the paragraphs below, where admittedly in each item I run the risk of assigning a view to a side in a manner which would not now be endorsed by that side. Nevertheless some explicit picture must be sketched if the case is to serve as a long term paradigmatic example for nuclear deterrence under asymmetric conditions. I will first argue the relevance of an unbiased perspective.

7.1 WHAT IS THE VIRTUE OF AVOIDING A BIAS?

I found it surprisingly difficult, however, to state precisely why it might be useful at all to avoid a bias (in the direction of the objectives of either side of a conflict) when presenting the conflict as a case study for nuclear deterrence theory.

Indeed when considered as a pure power struggle, a bias in the description does not matter so much, as it won't change the distribution of power. However, another line of argument is as follows. By avoiding a bias, a description can found which potentially renders the objectives of both sides as comprehensible perspectives for the opposite side. In addition I will assume that some form of mutual understanding is needed to engage in negotiations between both sides. And I assume that peaceful solutions including a managed denuclearisation of the weaker side are more likely than not to come about through negotiations.

Under these assumptions an observer who maintains a view of a conflict biased towards the perspective of a single side may thereby unknowingly ignore options for both sides to engage into negotiations. As a consequence of this ignorance the observer may happen to opt for a lower than plausible value of the subjective probability of the eventual occurrence of a peaceful and definitive solution of a conflict between two asymmetrically weaponised states.

7.2 POLITICAL ETHICS AND PERSPECTIVE

The following assumptions clarify that ethical or moral considerations do not stand in the way of the quest for impartiality.

Assumption 7.2.1. *Nuclear deterrence theory does not come with a ready made ethics* *of conflict and nuclear deterrence theory does not depend on any assumption of morality regarding the actors in an international conflict.*

Assumption 7.2.2. *There is no feature or property of the DPRK which, on apriori and obvious grounds, makes it significantly more problematic to the world community at large for the DPRK to be recognised as a nuclear-weapons state than it has been in the case of some of the already existing and recognised nuclear-weapons states.*

Assumption 7.2.3. *The KCW in the current phase (say 2017–2018) is focused on the princpled containment of nuclear proliferation as opposed to the emancipation of the DPRK to full military independence.*

Assumption 7.2.4. *Whether or not a world without nuclear weapons is to be preferred to a world with nuclear weapons is an open issue. Nevertheless:*

- *Maintaining operational nuclear weapons has been and still is ethically acceptable in principle, although this appreciation may change in thye future.*

- *Under which conditions the use of nuclear weapons is morally justifiable is far from clear and different nuclear-weapons states may entertain different views on that matter.*

- *As an act of faith, the assumption that nuclear deterrence stabilises the world (and has done so since 1945) is morally neutral.*[55]

Assumption 7.2.5. *Issuing a conditional threat about the use of nuclear weapons may be ethically permissible for the source of the threat even in cases where the actual keeping of the threat upon having been challenged (that is, the actual use of using these weapons) is considered unethical.*

7.3   PRIMACY OF ALTERNATIVE HISTORIES

It is impossible and unreasonable to insist that a joint perspective on past events is obtained first before elaborating views of both sides. Contradictory accounts of relevant history serve as a point of departure rather than as a conceptual problem in need of resolution. The following Propositions summarise the intended relation between views on the conflict and on its history.

Proposition 7.3.1. *Any attempt to work towards a joint (US and DPRK) account of the history of the Korean War and the subsequent KCW, in advance of further conflict resolution is bound to fail, and when working towards an impartial account one must be willing to think in terms of competing alternative histories.*

Proposition 7.3.2. *The plausibility of both positions outlined below can only be appreciated in the context of the respective and thoroughly disparate alternative histories entertained by both sides.*

7.4 TWO HYPOTHETICAL PERSPECTIVES ON THE KCW

It is impossible for an outsider to know what the DPRK leadership thinks, and it is also far from easy to find that out for the US. In this section I will provide two hypothetical perspectives on the KCW, one from a US point of view, and one from a DPRK point of view. The US case, just as the DPRK case, has been intentionally made as strong as it can be made, and no less.

These hypothetical views are in part based on an appreciation of recent events.[56]

Both perspectives consist of a listing of positions followed by a brief remark on what (hypothetically) the other side may think about that particular position. These perspectives are entirely subjective and are my own reconstructions (or guesses) of what may be in the minds of various politicians involved in the conflict.

I include a description of these perspectives in order to describe the ideological distance between both sides with some precision.

7.4.1 A HYPOTHETICAL PERSPECTIVE ON THE KCW FROM THE US POINT OF VIEW

Comparison of military strength.

The US can outperform the DPRK in all aspects of military operation and on all relevant battlefields both in conventional mode and with nuclear weapons used on both sides. A military victory, however, is likely to come with very high costs for the US and for one or more of its allies.

DPRK position: The DPRK agrees.

Nonproliferation in general.

The acquisition of nuclear weapons and corresponding capabilities of delivery by the DPRK contributes to nuclear proliferation. At the same time nonproliferation is a long standing UN endorsed objective and the US strongly adheres to nonproliferation as an overarching objective.[57]

Therefore the US will not accept the DPRK as a nuclear-weapons state on the long run, let alone as a thermo-nuclear-weapons state.[58]

Perry 1999 [45] summarises of US positions around 2000. The policies outlined in that paper have failed and the worries expounded in detail have materialised.

What was portrayed as possible in [45] has nowadays been achieved by the DPRK and the paper suggests that such achievements will pose grave security risks and must not be taken lightly.

The US claims to see no commitment of the DPRK to avoiding the spreading of military nuclear weapons technology to terrorist groups. If only for that reason nuclear proliferation to the DPRK constitutes an unacceptable risk for the US, and in the eyes of the US also for the world at large.

DPRK position: the DPRK is at least as able to manage its nuclear weapons in a responsible manner as any other recognised nuclear-weapons state.

Nonproliferation in the specific context.

The objection against the DPRK becoming a nuclear-weapons state consists of four components carrying comparable weights:

Principled nonproliferation.

Every further step of nuclear proliferation constitutes a serious problem and must be opposed by the world community at large. This objection applies to the DPRK but it is not specific for the DPRK, and is not depending on any actions or utterance from the side of the DPRK.

Domino theory.

If the DPRK becomes a recognised nuclear-weapons state there is no way to prevent the same happening to the ROK, Japan, Vietnam, Malaysia, Indonesia etc.

Micro proliferation.

Proliferation of nuclear weapon technology to the DPRK carries with it an unacceptable risk of further proliferation in the direction of terrorist organisations and networks throughout the world.

Risk of aggression and extortion.

The DPRK is (claimed to be) a rogue state which, assuming that it acquires the possession of usable nuclear weaponss, constitutes an immediate risk for a growing number of states throughout the world.

DPRK position: none of this is convincing, there is no evidence base for these views.

Options for reappraisal.

Nuclear deterrence theory as developed in the US in the second half of the 20th century had the USSR and the PRC as prototypical images of the enemy. By now it is acknowledged by the US that the political leaders in both states have acted responsibly thus far. A similar retrospective appraisal for the leaders of the DPRK cannot be ruled out in advance, but the potential prospect of that hindsight is not informing current strategic conceptions in the US.

DPRK position: reappraisal is indeed a likely scenario on the long run, perhaps after one or more regime changes in the US.

Mode and scope of deterrence.

The US policy towards the DPRK features double deterrence:

Conventional nuclear deterrence.

To deter the DPRK from military actions, and

Anti–proliferation deterrence.

Deterrence from developing and acquiring nuclear weapons with suitable corresponding delivery systems.

Moreover, anti–proliferation deterrence must established be so clearly that as a consequence also other states aspiring the acquisition of nuclear weapons will be deterred from moving in that direction in the future.

Moreover the US considers the DPRK to have been in breach of the framework agreed in 1994 which would bring North Korean development of nuclear weapons to a halt. A concise history of these events can be found in Litwak 2017 [36]. The US intends it to be made clear that such behaviour will meet fierce and decisive resistance.

DPRK position: this view underestimates the legitimacy of the DPRK's intention to take its own security in its own hands.

Regime change.

Regime change in the DPRK is not an objective per se for the US.

DPRK position: the DPRK agrees that regime change must not be a US objective, it does not trust the US in this matter, however, as its policies may change from president to president.

Comparative urgency.

The threat arising from the DPRK is considered to be more immediate and more in need of attention than climate problems and other ecological issues.

DPRK position: climate problems are real while the "Korean problem" is artificial and home made by the US.

Urgency of action.

Assume by way of a thought experiment that the DPRK intends to hit the US and

Japan in a dramatic manner. Now suppose that perfect international cooperation and coordination achieves a complete isolation of the DPRK, its borders becoming entirely closed. What will happen?

If the DPRK would (hypothetically) have the size and the strength of the PRC the answer to a corresponding question is simple because even an isolated PRC is able to compete with the rest of the world as a military power.

Will an isolated DPRK be able to set up its own computing industry and so on? Overestimating the solitary potential of the DPRK may have as a negative consequence, however, that a window of opportunity is missed, and the US prefers not to take that risk, whence there is a definite sense of urgency.

DPRK position: the DPRK will be able to strengthen its nuclear weapons systems regardless of external pressure. Therefore there is no risk of overestimating its solitary potential whence this argument for urgency of action is unconvincing.

Korean unification.

Options for unification of the DPRK and the ROK are listed in Gonsalves 2017 [27]. While claiming that the only feasible path towards DRPK–ROK unification requires a regime change in the DPRK which is brought about from inside, Gonsalves argues that DPRK–ROK unification would offer the best future for this part of Asia. The US view on unification has been adequately captured by Gonsalves.

Consistent with the analysis and suggestions of Chapman 2014 [21] the US intends to focus its cooperation with the ROK on security issues related to the DPRK, thereby avoiding to send confusing signals to other Asian states.

DPRK position: the DPRK is hopeful of Korean unification on the long run.

Regional responsibilities of the US.

The US has accepted a long term responsibility for the security of the ROK and Japan. Both states contribute to nonproliferation by abstaining from the development and deployment of atomic weapons. For the advancement of regional security the ROK and Japan maintain significant conventional military forces.

This arrangement has become increasingly problematic, assessed from the US perspective at least, because on the one hand regional security cannot anymore be protected in a credible manner by means of conventional weapons, while on the other hand a preemptive attack on the DPRK (when considered necessary by the US, for securing the positions of the ROK and Japan), is likely to have very unfortunate consequences for both Japan and the ROK.

In Hughes 2009 [31] the Japanese reaction to the security risk emanating from the DPRK was played down:

> Hence, at present the relatively weak North Korean nuclear threat is only sufficient to force Japan to saber rattle and question its anti-nuclear taboos, although in the future any potential for a growing North Korean nuclear capacity and perceived decline in the US defensive commitment might cause a more serious reconsideration of Japan's stance.

According to the US, by now the positions of Japan and the ROK need to be less relaxed.

DPRK position: such are the consequences of not having worked towards a peace treaty with the DPRK for over 65 years.

Learning from past failures.

Past US administrations have failed to contain the military development of DPRK. This unfortunate outcome must not be taken for granted, however, by the current administration, and not by forthcoming administrations.

The US is aware that in no previous stage have the ROK or Japan been willing to endorse a US initiated war with against DPRK in order to prevent nuclear proliferation to the DPRK.

DPRK position: learning from past failures is important, avoiding new failures is even more important.

Lessons taken from the Iraq war.

When initiating the war in Iraq in 2003 the US knew that it might err on the side of risk avoidance by assuming that Iraq was developing WMDs which in fact it was not. Harvey 2008 [29] explains in detail how this misunderstanding permeated all sides of the US political establishment as well as a majority in the UN. Iraq on the other hand additionally contributed to this misunderstanding by pretending that it was in command of WMDs, which it did in order to deter Iran from another war effort. The US, however, understood too late that it was not itself the target of these (deceptive) threats. Besides the war having been fought on the basis of invalid information in hindsight, the US has underestimated the complexity of a regime change in Iraq as well as the long term cost of the Iraq war.

After the Iraq war the US has preferred to err on the side of accepting risks by not taking military action earlier against WMD development in DPRK. But the fact that the US is late provides no justification for the US to ignore the problem at this late stage.

Nowadays the US considers the decision to declare war to Iraq to have been mistaken. The Iraq war was motivated as a necessary method to guarantee non-proliferation of weapons of mass destruction. The development and deployment of such weapons, however, turned out not to have been on the agenda of Iraq in those years.

The US has been reluctant to engage in a second war aiming at the prevention of proliferation. As a consequence, it may now appear that the US policy towards the DPRK provides too little pressure too late.

DPRK position: the Iraq war made the DPRK aware if imminent risks, upon which it took action. The opportunity for a successful attack by the US on the DPRK, which has existed indeed, is gone.

Brinkmanship endorsement.

The DPRK, the ROK, Japan and the US may find incentives for acts of so-called brinkmanship (Schelling 1960 [54], Nalebuff 1986 [41]). Showing brinkmanship involves deliberately running an increased risk of a nuclear war which might arise by either accident, or by mistake, or on purpose. The game theory of Nalebuff 1986 [41], however, speaks against the validity of assuming such "simplistic" impact assessments in terms of highly subjective probability changes.

The US acknowledges a potential for the productive use of brinkmanship in its relations with the DPRK.

DPRK position: the DPRK agrees with the potential relevance of brinkmanship.

The opponent's track record.

The DPRK has a track record of issuing conditional threats in the direction of the US, the ROK and Japan. Notwithstanding conditions that amount to the occurrence of "aggression" from the side of the US, the ROK or Japan, these threats are considered unacceptable by the US and by its allies.

On August 8, 2017 the DPRK has announced a plan (issued a threat) to simulate an attack on Guam by sending 4 missiles towards its proximity, an action that may be forthcoming within a few months.[59] The US is deeply concerned about such threats.

DPRK position: both sides have issued threats that the other side disapproves of.

The Korean war.

The DPRK performed a well-prepared attack on South Korea on June 25, 1950. A declaration of war was not issued, and the task to end this undeclared war, beyond the stage of the 1953 armistice, cannot be moved to either the US, the ROK, or both. Instead that task requires a strong commitment from the DPRK.

DPRK position: the history of the Korean war was different, and so are the consequences for working towards a lasting peace treaty.

Responsibility of other states.

The US holds each state which has been facilitating, either openly or covertly, the DPRK to import components of nuclear weapons technology and delivery systems, responsible for the current adverse and necessarily temporary status of the DPRK as a nuclear-weapon state.

The US calls on the entire world community outside the DPRK to steer by all means towards a quick, definite, enduring, and verifiable limitation of the DPRK's military nuclear capabilities.

DPRK position: the DPRK disagrees with these US objectives.

Failure of diplomacy.

The US feels that conventional diplomacy has proven ineffective against the DPRK. The US calls to all parties who are involved in the KCW, either directly or indirectly, to subscribe to this viewpoint and to draw the following conclusions that follow from it:

1. it is not an option for the US to avoid the use of conditional military threats at this stage,

2. at some stage unconditional military threats may need to be issued by the US against the DPRK,

3. military action against the DPRK cannot be ruled out, even if the US has to act alone and ultimately if the US must act without the support of the UN,

4. the scope of military actions performed by the US and its allies against the DPRK cannot be limited in advance.

DPRK position: the DPRK agrees that US Korean policies have failed, but the listed conclusions don't follow from that observation. Better policies are needed for the US.

Sprinting considered harmful.

Narang 2017 [40] provides a classification of processes for the development of nuclear weapons, referred to as nuclear acquisition theory. In [40] the step from weaponisation to delivery technology, in particular to ICBM delivery capability is not included. Nevertheless it is plausible to contemplate an extension of nuclear acquisition theory so as to include the acquisition of delivery systems and then it appears that, for such developments, the DPRK complies with the criteria which are mentioned as indicative for so-called sprinting in [40]. As Narang indicates, external economic pressure as well as potential military pressure both serve as incentives for sprinting.

The sprinting style development of ICBM capability by the DPRK triggers a stronger negative reaction from the US than the slow an cautious development and testing of nuclear weapons has done in the past.

DPRK position: the DPRK needed sprinting in order to have nuclear weapons delivery technology in place. Otherwise the risk of a preemptive strike by the US would have been unacceptable.

Dealing with the status quo.

As long as the DPRK maintains and develops nuclear weapons as well as delivery systems for these the US, the ROK, and Japan, feel free to deploy the newest ABM systems in the ROK and in Japan.

DPRK position: the DPRK agrees with this position.

Clarification of strategy.

Gray 1979 [28] (p62) wrote in connection with the relation between the US and the USSR:

> Incredible though it may seem, it has taken the United States' defense community nearly twenty–five years to ask the two most basic questions of all pertaining to nuclear deterrence issues: these are, first, what kinds of threats should have the most deterring effect upon the leadership of the Soviet state?–and, second, should pre–war deterrence fail, what nuclear employment strategy would it be in the United States' interest actually to implement?

Remarkably, 40 years later, these observations still apply to the antagonistic relation between the US and the DPRK: with some delay the US must, and will, in accordance with [28] determine what it means to win a war with the DPRK and the US will make up its mind on how to fight such a war.

DPRK position: the US is late in its realisation of the depth of its conflict with the DPRK, and it will need new ideas about its solution.

Conceivable positive outcomes of the conflict.

Besides a variety of possible negative outcomes, the conflict with the DPRK has either of two peaceful positive outcomes and an important objective of US policies will be to avoid arriving at some kind of compromise in between:

1. To negotiate successfully with the DPRK towards denuclearisation of the DPRK in return for adequate guarantees of its territorial security and political integrity.

2. To force the DPRK with the help of the PRC and Russia to stop further development and deployment of nuclear weapons, nuclear weapons delivery systems, and protection of those weapons and systems against current and forthcoming counter attack options and moreover to dismantle its currently operational nuclear weapons and delivery systems.[60]

3. To keep a long standing stalemate with DPRK allowing the build-up together with South Korea and Japan of extensive ABM systems, as well as the capability of a counterforce strike against DPRK.[61]

DPRK position: the DPRK does not rule out option 1, the DPRK has no faith in option 2, and the DPRK expects that option 3 will make it win the conflict simply by not losing it.

Parity rejected as a perspective.

The DPRK has stated that it intends to acquire military parity with the US. The US considers this objective to be unreasonable view of the relative positions and sizes of both states. The US is determined to see to it that only very few states achieve military parity with the US, the DPRK not being one of these states.

DPRK position: achieving military parity with the US is a legitimate objective for the DPRK.

A perpetual draw rejected as a perspective.

Following the terminology of Nalebuff 1988 [42] the DPRK might aim at so-called minimal nuclear deterrence. In 1988 it was already difficult to explain in detail what constitutes minimal nuclear deterrence and how to bring that state of affairs about. Some 40 years later it may have become unfeasible to provide a practical definition of minimal nuclear deterrence. Nalebuff 1988 begins with:

> In thinking about the nuclear arms race, the terminology can be counterproductive. Calling it a race suggests winners and losers. But unlike a footrace, an arms race can end with the outcome being left unresolved. How far must the race be run before both parties agree to a perpetual draw?

Although the US is not able to provide a precise answer on this classic question, the US is not willing to acknowledge a perpetual draw with the DPRK.

DPRK position: the DPRK works towards a perpetual draw or an even better outcome.

7.4.2 A HYPOTHETICAL PERSPECTIVE ON THE KCW FROM A DPRK POINT OF VIEW

I have made an attempt to represent the DPRK case as strong and convincing as possible, at least to my own understanding, irrespective of the question whether or not these arguments are used, or agreed with, or considered worth of contemplation by DPRK politicians. Just as the US case, the DPRK case is as strong as it can be made, and no less. It must be emphasised that this view is based on my own perception of a particular (alternative) history which supposedly supports this view. Some aspects of the hypothetical DPRK view are subsumed by its position statements regarding hypothetical US positions above.

Japanese occupation.

From 1910 till 1945 Japan occupied Korea, and Japan has since then failed to compensate adequately for this episode. Therefore Japan owes Korea and must not join forces with the US against the DPRK.

US position: it is implausible to connect Japanese policies of entirely different episodes in this manner.

Post WW II attitude towards the DPRK.

After WW II and before the Korean War the UN was not treating North Korea and South Korea in a symmetric manner, in fact the UN acted as if only South Korea was a legitimate representative of Korea.

US position: this part of history has now become almost irrelevant.

The Korean War: first phase.

The Korean War broke out when South Korea with US support attacked the North on June 25, 1950. In self-defense North Korea then invaded South Korea and conquered Seoul within 3 days.

The DPRK sees a correspondence with the start of the war in Vietnam. The US claimed that two subsequent attacks on the USS Maddox in the Bay of Tonkin in 1964 took place, thereby triggering the war in Vietnam. But according to the DPRK the first attack was solicited deliberately by the Maddox which opened fire while the second attack was merely faked. These so-called attacks were construed into a rationale and a justification for launching an attack by US marines and for initiating bombing raids on North Vietnam. Moreover the faked attacks were used as a justification for subsequent and prolonged military action in Vietnam without the need of a formal declaration of war.

US position: the US denies this picture of past events.

The Korean War: second phase.

Due to massive and immediate support from the US, the progress of North Korea was halted, thus preventing the unification of both Koreas. Subsequently the North Korean position degraded and became precarious. Then, however, Chinese support terminated the options for a victorious outcome for South Korea and the US. However, also without Chinese support the US would have been driven back to the old borders with South Korea and beyond.

US position: the US agrees with the first part but does not believe that without Chinese support the DPRK would have been victorious.

US war crimes during the Korean War.

During the Korean War the US performed excessive bombing on North Korean civilian targets. The DPRK considers these bombings to have constituted war crimes. The world community failed to protect the DPRK against these war crimes, and has failed to condemn these in a later stage.[62]

US position: these bombings were needed and were adequate given the military technology of those years.

Peace treaty promised but not delivered.

The 1953 armistice included a Promise Theory a peace treaty would be sought without much delay. US internal politics, however, led to delay after delay in working towards a lasting peace in Korea.

No other country has ever been at war with the US for over 65 years. The stress which comes about when peace with the US is a vague memory of one's grand parents at best must not be underestimated.[63]

US position: the DPRK has an equal share in the excessive delay of the creation of a peace treaty.

Justification of the Korean War.

After WW II the former opponents of Japan have shown more respect for the integrity of Japan as an empire than for Korea as an autonomous state. An attempt had to be made by either side to reunite Korea and a war was justified for that purpose.

US reasoning that a capitalistic parliamentary democracy is morally superior to communist peoples democracies is biased and unconvincing. Peoples democracies have been and still are very successful.

US position: the US disagrees with any attempt at justification of the Korean War.

Korean Cold War.

Since the armistice there is a Korean Cold War (KCW). It is a significant achievement that the DPRK has been able to survive the many phases of the KCW. The population of the DPRK is very proud of this achievement.

US position: the US disagrees, as there is no way for the US to find out what the population of the DPRK thinks.

US opportunism concerning recognition of nuclear-weapons states.

For the US recognition of a state as a nuclear-weapons state seems a matter of political convenience unrelated to facts. The US knows Israel to be a nuclear-weapons state while publicly ignoring that fact. The DPRK claims to be a nuclear-weapons state, a generally recognised fact, and the US refuses to see things that way. This biased approach fails to convince the DPRK of the peaceful intentions of the US.

US position: the US disagrees, the US recognises facts.

US opportunism regarding weapons trading.

Samore 2002 [52] has outlined the opportunistic stand of the US towards missile development by the DPRK. During the Clinton administration the US was bothered about technological development of advanced missiles inside the DPRK and about the export of missiles by the DPRK. In those years the DPRK has contemplated exporting missiles to Iran, by no means a terrorist organisation, and a country to which the US had shortly before sold weapons itself.

The DPRK appreciates that the US is unhappy about the DPRK selling missiles to a state upon a regime change, even if the US has been selling weapons to that very state just before said regime change. But such transactions are misrepresented as the DPRK trading with terrorist movements, or even as the DPRK showing irresponsible behaviour. Indeed the DPRK trades with states that have fallen out of the US's favour.

Finally the Clinton administration made up its mind on setting, admittedly workable, priorities concerning negotiations about missile trade and development with the DPRK, only to see this opportunity to strike a deal entirely discarded after the regime change to the Bush administration. The DPRK has been taken consistent and pragmatic views during that period, but to no avail.

US position: the US admits and regrets that its policies have sometimes been less coherent. Such inconsistencies are now being removed, however.

The 1984 framework agreement.

According to the US assessment the DPRK fails to comply with the 1994 framework agreement. The DPRK disagrees. Party politics within the US repeatedly frustrated US compliance with the agreed framework and the DPRK had no other option than focus on its own security interests. The DPRK has also been accused of disregarding the NPT until its withdrawal from NPT in 2003. However the DPRK points out that most nuclear-weapons states have systematically ignored the intended objectives of NPT by not moving towards denuclearisation, and did so, treacherously, without withdrawing from the NPT. So there is no reason to qualify DPRK behaviour as being problematic in this regard. Farago 2016 [22] details how often the US has broken its own promises:

> Nevertheless, this episode must have taught Pyongyang an important lesson, namely that the US administration has a habit of backtracking on agreements and a deal is only the beginning of an arduous negotiating process. In other words: talking to the US is a waste of time, for the US talks are merely a way to misguide the opponent.

The attitude taken by the current US administration towards the highly significant nonproliferation agreement with Iran supports this observation. The DPRK finds confirmation in the international press: The New York Times wrote in an editorial on October 17 2017:

> The countries that negotiated the deal with Mr. Obama – Britain, France, Germany, China and Russia – also begged the White House to stick with it. But Mr. Trump demonstrated once again that he can't abide his predecessor's accomplishments, that he will not be persuaded by facts and that he places little or no value on the idea that honouring national commitments safeguards confidence in America's word. Why would North Korea negotiate with the United States over its nuclear stockpile when it sees how little store the Trump administration sets by diplomatic accords?

US position: the US disagrees with this picture.

The DPRK is a nuclear-weapons state and must be recognised as such.

Since 2006 DPRK is a nuclear-weapons state.[64] The role of its nuclear weapons can be compared with the nuclear weapons of NATO (or more precisely, the

US, the UK and France) around 1975: a vastly stronger Soviet Russian army, in conventional terms, was (believed to be) discouraged (deterred) from attacking Western Europe because even a small conventional attack might well lead to a large nuclear response from the side of NATO. The US grasps very well what role nuclear weapons play for the DPRK.

US position: the US accepts the fact that the DPRK is currently a nuclear-weapons state. The US, however, denies that this development was needed and also denies that it wil be useful in the future.

The US misuses its controversy with the DPRK.
Futter & Zala 2015 [25] perceive as the key problem for the US how to deal with DPRK on the short term and with China on the long run. These authors indicate that by improving missile defense systems in the ROK and Japan, as well as by improving other conventional capabilities, the US might at some stage turn out to acquire a first counterforce strike capability towards the PRC, which then might destabilise the region. The DPRK concludes from these considerations that, against its wishes, the DPRK is used as a pawn in a US strategic game towards the PRC.

US position: the US discards this view. Acquiring a first counterforce strike capability against the PRC is not a US objective.

The DPRK is a thermo–nuclear-weapons state.
Since September 2017 the DPRK claims to have advanced to the status of a thermo–nuclear-weapons state. Development of a hydrogen bomb has been a natural step for all nuclear-weapons states and so it has been for the DPRK. The DPRK is waiting for a recognition of these simple facts by the US.

US position: the US is not yet convinced of the thermo–nuclear military capabilities of the DPRK.

The DPRK is economically viable.
Admittedly the DPRK is a relatively poor country, and complaints are made that its military build-up makes the DPRK even poorer. However, according to Baek 2013 [5] the ROK experienced an economic boost from its participation in the Vietnam war as an ally of the US. There was no contradiction between the acquisition of military strength and economic growth for the ROK, and the same holds for the DPRK.

US position: the DPRK is in need of much better international relations in order to improve its economy.

Deterrence.

Nuclear weapons can only serve as a deterrent if the corresponding delivery methods are available.[65] As airplanes are increasingly vulnerable the DPRK must develop ICBMs and IRBMs that can be equipped with miniaturised nuclear warheads. The development of flexible missile technology is more difficult and expensive than the creation of nuclear weapons.

Only by mounting nuclear weapons on an IRBM capable of reaching Japan the fact that the DPRK is a nuclear-weapons state acquires significance in terms of deterrence.[66]

US position: the US agrees with these observations.

Need for adequate missile testing opportunities.

Any test of an ICBM or an IRBM by the DPRK necessarily involves launching a projectile in such a manner that it crosses Japanese territory, as otherwise it will run an unacceptable risk to hit the ground in one of the DPRK's neighbouring states, Taiwan, The Philippines, or Indonesia. It would be plausible and useful if Japan agrees with such test flight trajectories for which rules and constraints can be negotiated.

This plausibility stems from the fact that Japan's security is guaranteed by the US, a state which in turn constitutes a security threat for the DPRK. Only by developing ballistic missiles that may reach US mainland the DPRK can be convincingly protected against US aggression. Such missiles must be tested and any plausible test flight trajectory makes use of Japanese airspace or risks hitting other states.

US position: the US disagrees and considers it to be entirely plausible that Japan refuses to allow missile test over its air space.

Seoul is not a target of nuclear deterrence.

Only to have the option to destroy Seoul is not a credible second strike capability for the DPRK. It is unreasonable that the US stays at war for 65 years with the DPRK and for this extended period expects the DPRK to contemplate second strike options only against persons who speak the same language and who sooner or later ought to be incorporated in the same nation.

The DPRK has a recognised conventional second strike capability towards the ROK.[67] Therefore a credible nuclear deterrence by the DPRK targets either Japan or the US or both. Given that Japan supports the US, Japan is also a target for nuclear deterrence from the side of the DPRK. None of these observations indicate an aggressive attitude of the DPRK.

US position: the US agrees.

US unreliability.

The US tends to portray the DPRK as unstable and unpredictable. For the DPRK this US propaganda constitutes a misrepresentation of the current situation. The US now wants to reverse on (i) the deal with Iran, (ii) the Paris treaty w.r.t. global warming, (iii) trade treaties in North America as well as with several Asian countries. (iv) The US now applauds Brexit, which it adviced against only recently. The US is a rogue state, freely changing its views upon any regime change brought about by an election.[68]

The DPRK will avoid being drawn into negotiations with the US only find out in a later stage that the US is considering its own, pre regime change, signature to have become worthless.

US position: using the phrase regime change for democratic elections is incorrect. New leadership may change policies, that is the whole point of elections.

Unimpressed by US threats.

The DPRK is not worried by the rather aggressive words used by the current US President in relation to its antagonism with the DPRK, though it preferred the more careful approach for choosing his words that was taken by his predecessor.

Both the US and the DPRK make use of wordings that tend to frighten an audience unaware of the literature of nuclear deterrence. Moreover:

- The DPRK appreciates that when speaking of military options the US can only speak in terms of highly destructive options, and that by doing so the US implicitly acknowledges the adequacy of the DPRK's nuclear deterrence for preventing small or medium scale military actions against it. In other words, by speaking in terms of massive destruction of the DPRK rather than in terms of smaller scale military operations against it, the US implicitly acknowledges that the DPRK is a viable nuclear-weapons state.

- Without presuming an effective and reliable second strike capability of the DPRK, immune against any US led counterforce strike, why would the US refrain from contemplating limited acts of aggression in order to increase pressure on the DPRK? That state of affairs is informed by classical literature on nuclear deterrence under the hypothesis that the DPRK is in the possession of credible nuclear deterrence already.

- The principal conceptual difficulty of nuclear deterrence theory has been and still is the conception of scenarios or strategies, for either side involved, in which the use of nuclear weapons is conceivably a rational action. This problem is no less grave for a very powerful nuclear-weapons state than it is for a state with a limited nuclear strike capability. The DPRK appreciates that there is no obvious, let alone evidence based, way for the US to deal with this problem, just as there is no obvious way for the DPRK to deal with such issues.

- That the US tries to progress by way of uttering drastic conditional threats is merely an application of a strategy dating back at least to the work of Schelling 1966 [55] and Powell 1985 [46]. The DPRK relies on the same views. It should be noted that according to the counterintuitive suggestions made by Powell, it is mistaken to assume that minimising the chance that a nuclear conflict arises by accident or after a political failure must be the highest priority for all parties involved.

- The threat that the US will fire at ballistic missiles launched by the DPRK even if there is no significant expectation that a missile will reach US territory is unproblematic for the DPRK.

  The US (and Japan) should feel free to attack each missile sent by the DPRK which is halfway Japan or beyond. An attack on a DPRK missile, successful or not, will not be understood by the DPRK as constituting an act of aggression against the DPRK. Damage caused by debris after such an attack is a responsibility of the attacker, however, and moreover, in case of a test, the DPRK is willing to pay for damages that might be caused by failures for which DPRK is solely responsible. Protocols for an orderly arrangement of these ideas will be useful and might be negotiated with priority.

US position: the US agrees with these views though not in public.

Entitlement to nuclear self-defence.

The DPRK holds that each nation which is unable to escape from a state of war for over 50 years is entitled to nuclear self-defense. The DPRK fails to see why it is a high priority for the UN to take away its nuclear weapons, given that it has not been an equally high priority to ensure lasting peace.

The DPRK notices that the UK and France have developed nuclear weapons and corresponding delivery systems under much less threatening circumstances than the DPRK is enduring.

US position: the US considers the objective of nonproliferation to be so important that these seemingly reasonable arguments put forward by the DPRK must take second place.

Alignment with the PRC must not be taken for granted.

Although the PRC has been supportive of the DPRK in many phases of its existence, the PRC has also indicated not to accept the DPRC as a nuclear-weapons state on the long run.[69] This important fact is indicative for the difficult position of the DPRK while it does in no way undermine its determination to acquire credible nuclear deterrence against the US.

US position: the US agrees.

Quality of arguments.

Commenters regularly suggest that the US must compromise with the DPRK thereby accepting that the DPRK has become a nuclear-weapons state in view of, and because of, the military capabilities the DPRK has already obtained.

This view is wrongheaded and the quality of the arguments brought forward by the DPRK ought to be appreciated more highly instead.

US position: the US does not comment on comments.

Impact of the Crimean War.

The Russian capture of power in the Crimea constitutes a problem for the NATO and its allies. By taking control over the Crimea Russia has violated article 1 of the Budapest memorandum (signed December 5, 1994) which came with the decision by Ukraine to subscribe to nonproliferation and to dismantle the nuclear weapons capability which Ukraine had inherited from the Soviet Union. The Ukrainian nuclear weapons system was in disarray and its modernisation would have been unaffordable for Ukraine. A major problem highlighted by the Crimean crisis, however, is that a treaty in which nuclear disarmament was coupled with assurances of territorial integrity turned out to be violated within 20 years. Why should the DPRK trust a similar agreement about its denuclearisation?

Russia has put forward arguments to justify its actions. These arguments, however, have failed to convince Ukraine, the EU member states and the NATO members. A double-bind exists: the US cannot accept the status quo in the Crimea without loosing ground regarding the credibility of what it may offer to the DPRK in return for its required denuclearisation. And at the same time the US needs Russia to impose sanctions on the DPRK.

In terms of promises, the Budapest memorandum constitutes a bundle of promises to which the US has subscribed. Is the US expected to enforce the keeping of such promises when another signatory does not? It is worth noticing that the PRC has carefully avoided being caught by the same paradox by signing a differently phrased agreement with Ukraine. In any case, if at some stage the DPRK is (hypothetically) proposed to sign a treaty in connection with nuclear disarmament and a transition to nonproliferation, the wording of the treaty regarding territorial guarantees will be need more scrutiny (and explicit guarantees) than it was given in the case of Ukraine in 1994.

US position: the US agrees.

7.5   EXTRACTING AN IMPLICATION FOR THE KCW?

The main conclusion I draw from these descriptions is that in my view it is definitely conceivable that the US and the DPRK each arrive at some form of appreciation of the opponent's position and that this happens to such an extent that a negotiated solution becomes possible. A negotiated solution may range from the US accepting the DPRK as a nuclear-weapon state to the DPRK accepting and implementing denuclearisation.

CHAPTER 8

DETERRENCE UNDER ASYMMETRIC CONDITIONS

I will first start with listing sone outlines of threats that may be plausibly issued under asymmetric conditions.

8.1 OUTLINE LEVEL THREATS FOR UNEQUAL STRENGTH

Here are some promises and threats which may be issued by a superior state A to a weaker state P. I assume that military superiority is primarily a matter of the advancement of military technology and the availability of sophisticated weapons systems, and is only marginally depending on numbers of armed forces.

monitoring flights by drones plan:
> A promises P that A will (only once or regularly) overfly the territory of P for intelligence purposes and will do so with drones. When such drones are attacked these wil operate in self defence, but will not attack either surface to air missile launching installations on the ground, or P's aircraft.

monitoring flights plan:
> A promises P that A will (once or regularly) overfly the territory of P for intelligence purposes, and will do so with ordinary military airplanes. When its aircraft are attacked these wil operate in self defence, but will not attack either surface to air missile launching installations on the ground, or P's aircraft.

first strike plan:

A (unconditionally) threatens P to perform a full first strike.

It is unlikely that a first strike is promised with a large scope, in particular it is to be expected that civilians or military staff of P will not be in scope of the promise, and that the strike is carried out with some element of surprise.

first strike plan p:

A (unconditionally) threatens P to perform a limited first strike following plan p to be executed at some unspecified later moment.

Example:

the US may issue the unconditional threat to the DPRK, that it will at some stage perform a limited attack on a specific type of artillery unit while leaving open which particular unit is to be chosen as a target.

conditional first strike plan with deadline t:

A conditionally threatens P to perform a full first strike unless A sees to it that condition C is avoided before time t.

Example:

In the case of US versus DPRK, the US may for instance promise to perform a significant first strike on DPRK unless DPRK begins with dismantling its nuclear weapons systems before time t.

weak conditional first strike plan:

A conditionally threatens P to perform a full first strike unless P makes a visible and credible attempt to see to it that condition C is avoided and does so before a deadline stated by A.

Example:

In the case of US versus DPRK, the US may for instance promise to perform a significant first strike on DPRK unless DPRK indicates its intention to begin with dismantling its nuclear weapons systems before a specified deadline.

counter strike plan p on attack a:

if P attacks A with an attack of the form a then A will retaliate with plan p.

Given the fact that A is stronger than P, the retaliation plan p need only be such that P is discouraged from repeated attacks of the form a on the long run. Moreover the plan p is plausibly such that it makes use of the superiority of weapons systems of A.

Example: 1

In the case of US versus DPRK a promise might be: if DPRK sends a missile that crosses the Pacific halfway in the direction of the US, the US will destroy within 15 minutes the site from which the missile was launched in such a manner that collateral damage will be confined to a radius of 5 km from the location of the launcher. If the launcher is mobile the distance it has moved since launching is added to this tolerance. Damage to DPRK property inflicted beyond that distance will be considered erroneous and the DPRK will be financially compensated for such damage.

Example 2:
I will assume that the US has already made the promise that all DPRK submarines will be under permanent surveillance of underwater hunter killer drones, which can at any time destroy each of these submarines.

Now the US may promise the DPRK that the destruction of all of its submarines will be performed immediately as soon as any missile launched from a DPRK site comes at a distance of 500 km or less of US mainland, or within 50 km of Guam.

8.2 MUTUAL NUCLEAR QUASI-DETERRENCE

I propose to label the state of affairs of the KCW during the summer and autumn of 2017, however unstable it may turn out to be, as a state of asymmetric mutual nuclear quasi-deterrence between the DPRK and the US joint Japan and the ROK.

A state of mutual nuclear quasi-deterrence is a particular state of asymmetric nuclear deterrence between two states, however, subject to several adaptations:

Power asymmetry.
There is a manifest asymmetry in that one of the sides is much stronger in all parameters of military importance than the other side.

Recognition asymmetry.
The stronger side is a generally recognised nuclear-weapons state, its status as such is uncontested. The weaker side is a de facto nuclear-weapons state though missing universal recognition as such in the sense of the NPT.

Recognition rejection.
The stronger side rejects and actively opposes the perspective that the state of equilibrium will evolve into a classical case of mutual nuclear deterrence on the basis of MAD (mutually assured destruction), or on the basis of a more advanced phrasing of mutual deterrence. The stronger side has promised that the weaker side will reverse on its nuclear weapons ambitions.

Recognition aspirations.

The weaker side has promised that it will become a recognised nuclear-weapons state which is able to deter all potential attackers. The weaker side has promised that it will not dismantle its nuclear weapons.

Medium term uncertainty of risk.

It is not clear to any side involved to what extent an armed conflict with the weaker side will bring with it the risk of a damaging nuclear weapons exchange which both sides have all reasons to fear.

Unilateral experience of successful deterrence.

The weaker side claims that the very fact that its opponent is not attacking proves that its own nuclear deterrence is working. The stronger side disputes that claim.

Medium term convergence to a stable status quo.

Without significant events, including a war, it is expected that the status quo of asymmetric nuclear quasi-deterrence spontaneously evolves into a different status quo in a time span of say 15 years. For this evolution different possible futures may be distinguished:

1) Denuclearisation (the weaker side gives in).

The weaker side ends up dismantling its nuclear weapons.

2) The stronger side obtains structural and lasting advantage (a draw).

The stronger side may be able to obtain a decisive and enduring advantage, for instance by

- building and deploying 10 new ABMs for each single new and weaponised ICBM or IRBM which the weaker state is able to construct and deploy,
- significantly improving its first counterforce strike capabilities (perhaps using killer robots),
- by means of sophisticated covert activities within the weaker side's territory,
- perhaps by blocking the acquisition of modern IT equipement, or item by simultaneously drowning the weaker side in a sea of irrelevant data which it deems necessary to store and analyse, so that its datascience capabilities are impaired by lack of database capacity, and by
- systematically slowing down the technological progress of the weaker side in all relevant areas.

3) Fluctuating chances (extended uncertainty).

The tide goes up and down repeatedly with the weaker side obtaining a credible second strike capacity in some phases and the stronger side regaining a credible first counterforce strike capability in other phases. However, after some time the stronger side wins, there is a draw, the weaker side wins, or the weaker side obtains parity,

4) Weaker side nuclear breakout (the weaker side wins).

A status quo of asymmetric but mutually recognised nuclear deterrence. In other words: the weaker side succeeds in developing a credible and durable second strike capability. This outcome is plausible as developing attack technology is considered less demanding than developing defensive systems in combination with sophisticated counterforce strike capability.

5) Parity (power balance harmonisation).

The weaker side obtains nuclear parity.

6) Reversal (power balance reversal).

The originally weaker side has become stronger than the originally stronger side, which is and remains a nuclear-weapons state.

7) Reverse denuclearisation (the stronger side gives in).

The originally stronger side is overpowered and gives in and denuclearises.

Periodic phases of crisis.

There is a latent and periodically acute sense of crisis in view of the facts that the stronger side has manifestly not yet reached its objectives.

The status quo of quasi-deterrence ends once there is an international agreement on a stable future state of affairs which puts an end to the mentioned uncertainties and which guarantees stability for more that 15 years to come.

The following proposition conveys the claim that in the context of the KCW at the time of writing of this monograph the notion of mutual quasi-deterrence applies.

Proposition 8.2.1. *The DPRK and the US are (as of mid 2017) in a status quo of asymmetric mutual nuclear quasi-deterrence, with the US constituting the stronger side and the DPRK playing the role of the weaker side.*

By consequence I hold that:

Proposition 8.2.2. *It is not the case (mid 2017) that the US (with its allies ROK and Japan) and the DPRK are in a phase of (ordinary) mutual nuclear deterrence.*

Whether or not the current equilibrium will, without drastic changes or even a war, evolve towards a status quo of (recognised and enduring) mutual nuclear deterrence is a difficult assessment which depends on many factors, and which I can at best assert positively with a subjective probability of 50%, i.e. I simply don't know, as it cannot be ruled out at all that the DPRK is sufficiently large and self-supporting to hold out an extended episode of isolation and trade boycotts and still acquire a nuclear breakout, to use a phrase taken from Litwak 2017 [36].

8.3   A COMMON SENSE INITIAL VIEWPOINT

I will phrase a well-known viewpoint which has been clearly outlined in Roy 2017 [49], in the following proposition:

Proposition 8.3.1. *(Common sense initial viewpoint.) The US cannot plausibly prevent the DPRK from obtaining effective methods of intermediate range and long range delivery of its nuclear weapons. Accordingly there is no military option available to the US against the DPRK which might change that state of affairs and for which the expected costs are acceptable.*

I will label Proposition 8.3 the common sense initial viewpoint. I use the phrase common sense for two reasons: first of all the idea that nuclear weapons capabilities once obtained by a state are there to stay underlies much of the conventional talk about nuclear deterrence and nonproliferation, and secondly because this point of view is widely reflected in the international press.

The common sense initial viewpoint entails the negation of Proposition 8.2.2 and moreover it is incompatible with Proposition 8.2.1 because it takes for granted a form of certainty about the future development which is explicitly not taken for granted in Proposition 8.2.1 the definition of asymmetric mutual nuclear quasi-deterrence.

The one and only argument given by Roy for the initial viewpoint is that expected costs to the ROK would be unacceptable, and the potential capability of the DPRK to effectuate a strike on Japan or on the US would not even change the calculation. Moreover, the circumstances arising from a forthcoming recognition of the DPRK as a nuclear-weapons state, would not be much different from the present status quo, not a game-changer in Roy's words (see also Roy 2016 [47]). Consistent with Waltz 1981 [66], Roy suggests that the US might best accept a development where the DPRK grows into a recognised nuclear state and hope and expect nuclear deterrence to stabilise the US DPRK relations in the same manner as nuclear deterrence has been successful until now between other pairs of nuclear-weapons states.

The suggestion that the US and its allies have no realistic military options usable to force the DPRK to dismantle its nuclear weapons has much support in public media throughout the world. If one accepts this viewpoint then it follows that each promise or threat, either conditional or unconditional, made by the US towards the DPRK which involves military actions, can only introduce unnecessary risks without delivering any advantage, and ought to be avoided for that reason. It follows from these assumptions that the role of promises and threats in this phase of the KCW is cosmetic at best except for the "classical" promises and threats involved in nuclear deterrence.[70]

8.4 REJECTING THE COMMON SENSE INITIAL VIEWPOINT

The common sense initial viewpoint corresponds, in terms of its consequences, with the position of the DPRK and therefore it may be considered biased. However I consider the problem with Proposition 8.3.1 not to lie in its correspondence with the positions of the DPRK but in the absence of compelling arguments for it.

The viewpoint that the US has no military options against the DPRK, and that corresponding promises and threats are bound to be vacuous, is to some extent biased against the US which is generally understood to be far stronger and to be much better equipped than the DPRK in all possible dimensions of military operation. It is implausible to assume without scrutiny that the US and its allies adopt, as if it were a logical necessity Proposition 8.3.1.

I assume that exchanges of conditional and unconditional promises involving the use of either specified or unspecified military options and threats between the major players in the Korean Cold War may well be vacuous, but definitely need not be vacuous. Insisting in advance and without significant scrutiny that there is no military option (for either party) available which may significantly change the current status quo of armistice between the DPRK and the protagonists of the UN coalition that fought the Korean War, takes too many assumptions about the theory and practice of nuclear deterrence for granted.

Once the existence of military options for either side is not ruled out, promises and threats involving such options, or the perspective thereof, will play an important role. A justification of issuing such conditional or unconditional promises and threats will require a modern perspective on nuclear deterrence in general and on the KCW in particular which deviates from Proposition 8.3.1. It follows that promises and threats involving military options and in the context of KCW merit close attention. This holds for promises an threats which have been issued in practice by either side as well as for promises and threats which may or might be contemplated by either side.

Here is an example of a threat (as communicated by the Independent) issued by the US President on September 26, 2017:

> "We are totally prepared for the second option, not a preferred option" Mr
> Trump said at a White House news conference alongside Spain's Prime
> Minister Mariano Rajoy. "But if we take that option, it will be devastating,

> I can tell you that, devastating for North Korea. That's called the military
> option. If we have to take it, we will"

By rejecting Proposition 8.3.1 the path is open for formulating some working hypotheses of this monograph:

1. promises and threats involving military options need not necessarily be considered as being either vacuous and merely knowingly hiding the absence of military options or being irresponsible by potentially increasing the risk of a war (as the only plausible side-effect),

2. that such promises and threats (from either side of course) may, at least conceivably, in certain conditions be sensible and effective, and

3. that promises and threats involving military options need not necessarily involve full military and nuclear strikes but may also involve limited operations involving tactical nuclear weapons as well as purely conventional actions.

8.5　Mack's thesis

For the strategy of A to work it is essential that it is able to keep focused on the same course of action for an extended period of time. Now the analysis of Mack 1975 [38] comes into play: for the weaker side P there is much more at stake than for A, and its determination may stay unchallenged during a protracted phase of stress, while the stronger side A needs to keep its internal political act together. Once the antagonism against P becomes politically unpopular it may become very difficult for A to keep the basic promise of permanent pressure towards nonproliferation w.r.t. P. Mack writes:

> Above all, Vietnam has been a reminder that in war the ultimate aim must
> be to affect the will of the enemy.

This ultimate aim may be just the same in the case of a cold war. Adding to the difficulties of A is that A also may have to deal with nonproliferation issues elsewhere and may be under pressure from inside to operate consistently, and A's regime changes for instance due to a succession of regular elections may make it harder for A to keep its policy focused on objectives set by a previous US administration.[71] The approach of Mack 1975 [38] seems to fit better with the asymmetric battle of promises and threats than the more recent approach of Arreguín–Toft 2001 [2] which takes the actual scenario's of physical warfare into account.

Using Mack's work on asymmetric conflict as a predictor for the outcome of the KCW one is led to predict that the DPRK will be victorious and will sooner or later achieve an irreversible nuclear breakout.

Chapter 9

Beyond the Korean Cold War: microattacks

In this Chapter and in the subsequent Chapters 10 and 11, I will discuss the potential rol of promises in an asymmetric conflict between nuclear-weapons states without suggesting any implication that these forms of promises and threats have any role to play, now or in the future, in the specific context of the KCW. The role of the KCW as a motivating case ends at this point in the work.

I will now assume that A intends to change the behaviour of P, with or without a regime change. For instance A may want P to dismantle its nuclear weapons or the delivery systems thereof.

Assuming that state A is much stronger than P, how can A make use of that advantage, except by having a full war against high cost? If P is able to raise the cost of a full war with A so high that a straight attack by A cannot be justified as a policy of A, the strength of A is of no help, and making A stronger won't be of much to it help either.

Below I will discuss several methods for exploiting military superiority and comment on the related use of promises and threats.

9.1 Microattacks

A is in need of actions and weapons that on the one hand will allow A to put pressure on P, while not inviting a full (first strike like) second strike from P. It seems that digital attacks are viewed as options which will not invite the use of weapons of mass destruction by way of retaliation. A must invest in military options against P that are on the verge of covert actions. Many such techniques can be imagined and here is not the place to discuss these in detail. However, a distinction can still be made: covert microattacks, that is microattacks taking place in secrecy and perhaps making use of weapons not known to P, and public microattacks, that is micorattacks which are carried out openly, perhaps after a preceding conditional or unconditional threat has been made. Obviously only public microattacks can be the subject of a preceding promise or threat.

9.2   SUB–PARITY PUBLIC MICROATTACKS

A conditional threat by A to perform a public microattack m_a^s can for instance take the following form: unless P promises to end its cyber attacks on other states including A and its allies before date d,[72] A will perform attack m_a^s. Moreover when P mounts a counterattack during m_a^s thereby potentially destroying the forces involved in the microattack, then A will respond with limited means only in order to avoid the local conflict spinning out of control. The microattack m_a^s has a sub–parity planning, that is a planning where parity with expected counter forces is not planned, which increases the chance for P to achieve a winning outcome of the resulting exchange. A high tech method for of m_a^s may limit the risk of loss of life for A while still allowing a reasonable chance of a positive outcome for P so that the incentive for P to retaliate with a full strike is kept low.

The idea of a sub–parity microattack is that it can conceivably be promised to P in such a manner that P can accept the promise by means of a counter promise to the extent that a proportional though super–parity strength response will be produced. Indeed, it seems to be a remarkable consequence of nuclear deterrence that nuclear states may agree on fighting with limited means and with a skewed distribution of military strength.[73]

If A is sufficiently strong there it may be possible to repeat attacks m_a for different targets, each time allowing a victorious outcome for P, thereby providing a disincentive for P to launch a significant counterattack, and still inflicting so much damage on P that in time P is fundamentally weakened so that it may contemplate the acceptance of desires as brought forward by A.

While a public exchange of promises and threats may precede and follow m_a, A may be involved in covert microattacks (not announced by means of threats with extensive scope) which may be difficult for P to detect and which for that reason are unlikely to lead to massive retaliation.

9.3   ACCEPTANCE BY A OF MICROATTACK THREATS ISSUED BY P

Another way in which A can make use of its strength is to provide a catalogue of promises each specifying limited strength response on conceivable microattacks or attempted microattacks of P. Having this catalogue available may have the effect that P is encouraged rather than discouraged from performing microattacks on A.

Being the stronger power A can deter P from military actions or provocations. The resulting stalemate, however, may not serve A's purposes. Therefore A may be better served with a policy to use promises and threats in such a manner that frequent small scale, and for that reason definitely conventional, military exchanges take place. In the limit A might be engaged in a full conventional war with P, in which according to the assumption of A's superiority, A would be victorious.

Yet another advantage of the use of microattacks preceded by threats to that extent by A, and of issuing promises of acceptance for microattacks that might be performed by P, with or without a preceding promise or threat to that extent, may be as follows: if A considers it advantageous to have verbal interaction with P without having formal talks with P on the terms determined by P, then frequently exchanging promises and threats in connection with microattacks may be helpful to that extent. By threatening with implausible or speculative microattacks (that is by issuing deceptive threats which) potentially a lot of publicity within A as well as within P may be achieved.

9.4   ISOLATION RESULTING FROM NON-VIOLENT MICROATTACKS

One particular form of microattacks consists of steps towards the isolation of P. Isolation of P may be sought by A concurrently with a spectrum of microattacks. One may imagine that A uses its power to move other states of P to refuse trading with P and to prevent trade with P with states that may not be influenced by A. On the long run that state of affairs may be detrimental to P. Will this form of trade boycott and isolation create a state from which the best option for P is to give in to the demands of A because the population of P cannot cope with the difficulties which are resulting? Or will the situation be such that on the long run P cannot keep the technology of its nuclear weapons systems up and running?

The situation is relatively simple: either the isolated position of P is sustainable for P on the long run and the isolation will be given up in due time, or P must admit, though perhaps not publicly, that the isolated position which it has arrived at is not sustainable.

In the latter case there are three options left, quite irrespective of the internal political structure of P: either (i) P gives in to the demands of A and effectuates a behavioural change, or (ii) P issues so clear threats of military aggression that A gives in and relaxes the isolation of P, or finally (iii) P starts a war with A and its allies in order to escape from strangulation, a war which brings for P with it the significant risk of being defeated, and as a consequence of defeat a high degree of destruction as well as a large number of military and civilian casualties.

It is customary in the West to assume that if P were a parliamentary democracy, P would opt for option (i) or perhaps for option (ii) rather than for the much more dangerous option (iii). For that reason a regime change in P might be helpful to make it agree with A's demands. This assumption is speculative at best[74]

Assuming that P is not inclined to surrender to the demands of A in view of its isolated position, the only the options (i) and (iii) remain open for it. A remarkable race condition arises: is P capable to acquire a reliable second strike on A after its position has become isolated, in such a manner that a credible threat for the ability of P to perform a a first strike towards A can be made for it.

9.5 STATE P ISSUES A THREAT BEFORE INITIATING MILITARY ACTION

Once state P is enduring extreme political and economic isolation and once P has arrived at the conclusion that (i) protracted isolation is unsustainable for itself, while (ii) in a military exchange it can inflict very serious damage to its opponent A, the military option becomes realistic for P. Now P may plausibly have the following preferences in decreasing order:

1. Threatening A with a small scale attack (as wel as the promise not respond moderately and in self–defense only to a defensive reaction from A, thus facilitating a winding down of the armed exchange when it takes place). Issuing this threat is meant to (i) demonstrate that from now on threats issued by P will be kept, and (ii) to point out to A that P sees no useful and peaceful means for conflict resolution.

2. Merely threatening A with a full scale military exchange with the effect that A openly and clearly withdraws its requirements on P and terminates its policy of isolation of P.

   A key difficulty with this option is: how to communicate the fact that this time threats won't be vacuous (how to make sure that the threat is effective in the sense of Paragraph 4.4 above).

3. To perform a small scale attack (after having threatened A with that action, though with the additional promise that a large scale attack need not follow as long as A responds in a moderate manner) on A in order to demonstrate that by now the military option has indeed become the preferred option for P to escape from the long term risk of economic strangulation.

4. To launch a full scale attack on A and its allies irrespective of the consequences thereof.

It seems rational for P to issue a threat in advance of any military action against A, in order to minimise the probability of a devastating overreaction by A.

9.6 STATE A ISSUES A THREAT BEFORE INITIATING MILITARY ACTION

For A the need to engage in military action arises if sustained economic boycott and isolation of P is unlikely to prevent P from achieving a durable a nuclear breakout in the terminology of Litwak 2017 [36]. Then A may see no alternative to mounting an attack. Now the attack is certain to be very costly for P and in the light of of the assumed superiority of P it does not make much difference if P receives an advanced warning that a serious attack is on its way. It follows that it is plausible for A to issue a (warning) threat of the impending attack. If A doubts that a threat wil be effective because too many of A's threats have not been kept, the A may first issue a threat for a limited attack, and the perform that attack in order to communicate to P that a threat of a full scale attack is not a deception, an awareness that P needs to have for A's threats to be effective.

CHAPTER 10

STRATEGIC PROMISES AND THREATS

I will now take into account the existence of additional states which serve as allies of the stronger state in a conflict about nuclear proliferation with a would be nuclear-weapons state.

I will assume the presence of two states B and C which are allies of A. B is a neighbour of P and can be attacked by P using conventional weapons, while C lies at a further distance from P though much closer to P than A. Attacking C by conventional means is hardly and option for P, but performing a nuclear attack on C may well be feasible option for P.

Rather than to list a long series of potential promises and threats I will consider a combination of a threats and promises for P, both involving B and C besides A which each are supposed to be maintained during an extensive episode and which together may characterise the position of a state. Looking at a few but durable promises and threats works as a simplification which may provide additional insight.

This part of the work is schematic and exploratory, as it is unlikely that in practice state P would confine its use of promises and threats to just a few each. The primary objective of this chapter is to illustrate how the language of Promise Theory extended with threats may be used as a specification method for the political state of affairs between antagonistic states and their allies, as well as for long term strategies of such states.

10.1 A THREAT AND TWO PROMISES FOR THE WEAKER SIDE

I assume that P is the weaker side in the conflict. The following combination of a threat and two promises brings about how P may try to keep the equilibrium state as long as possible in order to make as much progress as possible with its weapons development.

threat

name principal threat of deadly retaliation

short name ptodr

source P

body P will attack A, B, and C in the following manner:

- (if B was an ally of P until 7 days before the challenge took place) then the capital of B will be destroyed by means of conventional weapons irrespective of the loss of civilian lives; however, B will be allowed two days delay in order to evacuate the capital provided no attempt to a counterforce strike on the weapons systems and military units that P will need for this attack is made in between, (otherwise the attack will be performed without any further delay)

- (if C was an ally of P until 7 days before the challenge took place) the capital of C will be destroyed irrespective of the loss of civilian lives, C will also have three days to evacuate its capital, and another big city of C (yet undisclosed which one that will be) will be destroyed, and

- (if either B or C was an ally of A until 7 days ago) one large city on the mainland of A will be destroyed, and this will take place with the risk of much loss of civilian lives.

- (if neither B or C was an ally of A until 7 days ago) two large cities on the mainland of A will be destroyed, also with the risk of much loss of civilian lives.

target A

condition A (or B or C or any combination of these) performs an attack on P which is of one of the following forms:

- until 2 weeks ago B and C had not disconfirmed their alliance with A,

- a significant attempt to perform a counterforce attack on some of P's weapons systems,

- an attack on P with a significant number of civilian casualties,

- an attack which somehow resembles a previous attack by A (with or without its allies) on P and for which has P shown restraint by not retaliating, and for which P has announced that a second attack of a similar form would invite uncompromising retaliation by P.

qualifier +

deadline 14 days.

bias towards achieving a nuclear breakout for P.

(hidden) source credibility $Prob_T(condition, body) = 75\%$

(hidden) intended target credibility $Prob_S(condition, body) = 75\%$
(this is the target credibility which P seeks to install in the perception of A, B, and C).

scope A, B, and C (that is the political leaders and citizens of these states).

The principal threat of deadly retaliation must be seen in connection with the following principal promise of peaceful behaviour.

promise

name principal promise of peaceful behaviour

short name ppopb

promiser P

body P will not attack A, B, and C with weapons of mass destruction.

promisee A

condition A or B or C (or any combination of these) does not perform any attack on P which is of one of the following forms:

- a significant attempt to perform a counterforce attack on some of P's weapons systems,

- an attack on P with a significant number of civilian casualties,

- an attack which somehow resembles a previous attack by A (with or without its allies) on P and for which has P shown restraint by not retaliating, and for which P has announced that a second attack of a similar form would invite uncompromising retaliation by P.

qualifier +

bias towards achieving a nuclear breakout for P.

(hidden) source credibility $Prob_T(condition, body) = 100\%$

(hidden) intended target credibility $Prob_S(condition, body) = 95\%$
(this is the target credibility which P seeks to install in the perception of A, B, and C).

scope A, B, and C (that is the political leaders and citizens of these states).

The principal promise of peaceful behaviour coexists with the principal promise of proportional retaliation in response to minor aggressions.

promise

name principal promise of proportional retaliation on minor aggression

short name ppopr

promiser P

body P will respond to attacks of A,B, and or C with proportional though discouraging response.

promisee A

condition A or B or C (or any combination of these) does not perform an attack on P which is of any of the following forms:

- a very limited attempt to perform (or to experiment with) an attack on some of P's weapons systems which is som small in scope that it qualifies as a provocation rather than as a realistic counterforce attack,

- a limited attack on P with a very limited number of civilian casualties, which has been carried out without the intention to inflict damage to civilian life or property, and for which the attacker apologises without delay,

- an attack which somehow resembles a previous attack by A (with or without its allies) on P and for which has P shown restraint by not retaliating, and for which P has announced that a second attack of a similar form would again invite limited though discouraging retaliation by P.

qualifier +

bias towards achieving a nuclear breakout for P, and towards minimising the risk of the occurrence of a major military exchange by showing some robustness against minor aggression and provocation.

(hidden) source credibility $Prob_T(condition, body) = 95\%$

(hidden) intended target credibility $Prob_S(condition, body) = 50\%$
(this is the target credibility which P seeks to install in the perception
of A, B, and C).

scope A, B, and C (that is the political leaders and citizens of these states).

A rationale for this promise–threat bundle from the perspective of P is as follows:

Room for proportionality.
In case of minor attacks from A, B, and C it must be the case that P can react in a
proportional manner without diminishing the source credibility of the principal
threat of deadly retaliation.

Discouraging opportunistic behaviour of B and C.
From the outset it must pointed out by P to B and C that these states may have to
pay a high price for their loyalty to A. Disloyalty to A, however, must be promised
by these states to P in advance, if they want to be protected against retaliation
from P.

Protection of long term relations with B.
As B is a neighbour of P it is important for P to be able to have workable relations
with B on the long run and for that reason the population of the capital of B
is given the option to evacuate the capital, and to limit the number of civilian
casualties. Moreover only conventional weapons will be used for the destruction
of the capital of B so that rebuilding will not be frustrated by radioactive fall-out.

Deliberate creation of uncertainty for A.
The threat introduces significant uncertainty for A. In this respect a threat with a
nuclear attack is comparable to a threat involving an act of terror.

Winning by not losing.
With this single threat P intends to prevent A (with help of B and C) from attacking
P, with the ultimate aim to achieve a phase in which it is obvious for A and its
allies that it is useless and counterproductive to deny the presence of a credible
and durable second strike capability of P.

Restraint without commitment to nonviolence.
The impact of the threat towards A, B, and C is limited rather than maximal. But
obviously these states must take the risk into account that P reacts in a much more
forceful way because P has not promised to refrain from a more forceful reaction.

10.2 THREAT OF DEADLY RETALIATION

The policy for determining target credibility as discussed in Section 4.2.2 is not applicable in the case of a single phase of issuing promises and threats because there is no learning mechanism (for the target) based on a sequences of assessments for a trace of subsequent promises and threats.

In the single phase case a different approach may be useful. I will now focus on the principal threat of deadly retaliation, below abbreviated as *ptodr*. For this threat A is the target and P is the source, and the question is what can be said about the target credibility of this threat which I will denote with

$$Probability_A^{ptodr}(condition, body).$$

Now I assume that A makes an effort to estimate the source credibility (that is the credibility that P assigns to its own threat) of the threat *ptodr* and takes that same value, written

$$Probability_{P[A]}^{ptodr}(condition, body)$$

as its estimate for the target credibility as well.

In order to guess the source credibility of threat *ptodr* A assumes that this value is the product of the following three subjective probabilities (for A): (i) the ability of P to detect A's attack, (ii) the (existence of the) will of P to retaliate and (iii) the capability of P to do so successfully, and each of these values must be estimated by A.

$$Probability_A^{ptodr}(condition, body) =$$

$$Probability_{P[A]}^{ptodr}(condition, body) =$$

$$ProbabilityDetection_{P[A]}(condition) \cdot WillTo_{P[A]}^{body(ptodr)}(condition) \cdot$$

$$Capability_{P[A]}^{body(ptodr)}(condition).$$

For simplicity I assume that $ProbabilityDetection_{P[A]}(condition) = 1$. Moreover I will assume that that

$$WillTo_A^{body(ptodr)}(condition) = 95\%$$

as there is no reason for A to doubt the intention of P to defend its position by means of the actions as specified in the threat.

Estimating $Capability_{P[A]}^{body(ptodr)}(condition)$ is not easy for A, and such an estimate is likely to vary in time. At least the following aspects come into play for the quantification of the subjective probability (for A) of this capability:

1. Determination of $Capability_{P[A]}^{body(ptodr)}(true)$, i.e. the subjective probability (as estimated by A) that P is able to launch the specified counterattack. A counterattack involves sending so many missiles and artillery shells with sufficiently strong explosives and with sufficient precision that the projected destruction is likely to be achieved under the assumption that P has not yet been damaged by any preceding attack, that is the "condition" is assumed to be true in the absence of any provocation by A or its allies.

   $Capability_{P[A]}^{body(ptodr)}(true)$ is a measure for A's assessment of the capability of P to launch a successful (and for that reason referred to as deadly) first strike.[75]

   Now it may be assumed that ABMs will successfully intercept 50% of the incoming missiles and that only 5% of artillery shells can be intercepted.

2. The discount

$$\Delta_{condition}Capability_{P[A]}^{body(ptodr)}(true)$$

   on $Capability_{P[A]}^{body(ptodr)}(true)$ is A's estimate of the decrease of the subjective probability of P's first strike capability which can be achieved by A, (working together with B, and C) by means of a well planned first strike by A on P. Thus, by attacking P in counterforce mode, the capability for retaliation of P can be diminished, and the resulting consequence of a first strike on P may be understood as a discount on its capability to perform a first strike:

$$Capability_{P[A]}^{body(ptodr)}(condition) =$$
$$Capability_{P[A]}^{body(ptodr)}(true) - \Delta_{condition}Capability_{P[A]}^{body(ptodr)}(true).$$

3. The stage of development of defensive technology for A, B, and C against the weapons available to P.

4. The number of weapons that P is commanding.

5. The ability of P to keep in command of its forces and to initiate retaliation in spite of an attack by A and its allies (B and C).

Obviously all of this is rather difficult to quantify in a meaningful manner, but some qualitative remarks about that are made in the following Paragraph.

10.3   HOW P MAY INFLUENCE ITS CREDIBILITY IN THE EYES OF A

The purpose of P with issuing the principal treat of deadly retaliation is to avoid being attacked by A and its allies B and C. The key value which determines whether or not avoiding such an attack by means of the principal threat of deadly retaliation will be successful is $Q_A = Probability_{P[A]}^{ptodr}(condition, body)$. If Q_A is high then A strongly believes that P will successfully retaliate upon an attack by A, and if Q is low, then A believes that it can perform an attack on P without much risk. $C_A = Capability_{P[A]}^{body(ptodr)}(true)$ is the key parameter for A's determination of Q_A. Q_A is important for P and P may wish to influence its value in either direction.

P can influence Q_A both in upward and in downward direction in several ways:

- P may influence A such as to decrease Q_A by making A underestimate P's capabilities thus providing an incentive to set C_A too low. This may be done by profile weakening methods:

    - keeping military R&D progress hidden,

    - suggesting that real missiles are decoys,

    - making vehicles more visible to radar satellites than these will be in time of war,

    - let stealth technology operate in a non-stealth manner,

    - intentionally making weapons tests fail,

    - suggesting that disasters take place in its factories or store rooms,

    - intentionally testing techniques which have already been sufficiently mastered,

    - issuing threats that certain technologies will become available in coming years while in fact the same are already familiar for P and have been adequately weaponized,

    - trying to buy on the illegal weapons market technology which is already available to P, and doing so in a manner which transpires to A.

- P can try to induce A to set the value of C_A too high by profile boosting methods:

    - claiming achievements that have not yet been achieved,

    - secrecy about weapons tests, suggesting that failures have been successes,

    - proclaiming R&D targets which are far beyond the horizon of what P can achieve,

    - producing and deploying decoy weapons systems (so that the arsenal size appears too high).

- P can decrease $WillTo_{P[A]}^{body(ptodr)}(condition)$ by issuing novel peaceful promises and by overriding past unfriendly threats by novel less unfriendly threats.

- P can increase $WillTo_{P[A]}^{body(ptodr)}(condition)$ by retracting earlier peaceful promises and by issuing new and unfriendly threats.

10.4   POSITION, VELOCITY, MASS, AND MOMENTUM

P's development of weapons systems may at each moment be described by the following four parameters. A in turn will try to make educated guesses about these.

High end position: A qualification of the best technical level of achievement of P (the maturity of P) in a bundle of military technologies.

High end velocity:
A measure of the progress in position: how fast is P's military R&D making progress?

Mass:
The number of weapons (usable weapons systems) which as been produced and is available for use.

Momentum:
The overall quality and volume of upgrading per year to the latest available (to P) standards of the full range of relevant weapons systems.

10.5   DETERRENCE VERSUS PROVOCATION AND NET DETERRENCE

Provocation is the counterpart of deterrence, it is a qualification of the degree to which P produces incentives for an attack rather than deterrence of an attack. Provocation in this sense arises from developments in military capability only, not from military actions or threats issued by political or military leaders.

The quest for deterrence by P may, by itself constitute, or be understood by A to constitute, a provocation by P. Deterrence must be balanced with provocation. Net deterrence may be defined as:

$$Net\ deterrence = deterrence - provocation.$$

Deterrence by P is determined by (and correlates positively with) its high end position as well as its mass, while provocation is determined by (and correlates positively with) its high end velocity and its momentum.

P achieves best net deterrence by making A overestimate its mass and high en position and at the same time underestimate its high end velocity and momentum.

Using this terminology it seems that it is attractive for P to make A (and, perhaps more importantly, the civilian population of B and C) overestimate position and mass of its second strike force, and at the same time to make A (and the civilian population of

B and C) underestimate velocity and momentum thereof. Here the idea is that at each moment the population of B and of C are likely to be looking eagerly for any reasons to postpone the first counterforce strike by the joint forces of A, B, and C. Velocity and therefore momentum being near zero is potentially a very strong argument for delay.

10.6 THREATS AND PROMISES FOR THE DOMINANT SIDE

Assuming that A intends to force P into submission to the extent that it discontinues its nuclear weapons capability then A must find a strategy that may outsmart or outperform the threat plus two promises based strategy of P as proposed by the specification in Section 10.1.

Assuming that A and P are in a phase of asymmetric mutual nuclear quasi-deterrence, and assuming that P has issued the principal threat of deadly retaliation and the principal promise of peaceful behaviour, then the following four options for A seem to be exhaustive:

Giving in.
To accept P's ascendance to the rank of recognised nuclear-weapons states,

Counterforce attack.
To carry out a counterforce attack while accepting the adverse consequences for itself (as specified in P's threat), for B and for C, preferably choosing the right moment for that,

Sustained boycott and isolation.
To carry out a sustained boycott and isolation of P, in the absence of heavy use of force, which supposedly will make it impossible for P to achieve a nuclear breakout, (though admitting in private that a temporal phase of nuclear quasi-deterrence between A and P cannot be avoided), so that P will be forced to give up its nuclear ambitions in due time.

Sustained boycott and isolation with a full strike meta-promise.
To combine sustained boycott and isolation with admission that a surgical counterforce strike is not an option for A and the Promise Theory on the long run a conditional treat of a full scale attack on P will be issued.

The first option comes with a package or promises by A indicating that A won't try to punish P any further for its intention to become a powerful nuclear-weapons state.

The second option comes without promises and threats. Indeed a first strike (in this case a counterforce strike) to which a side (here A) is unconditionally committed is likely to be carried out (by A) by surprise, and the element of surprise may be spoiled by issuing a promise or threat in advance.

The third option is the only option which combines the perspective of success for A with the option to avoid a disastrous war. The promise below expresses in detail what state A is in if the third option is chosen. I have tried to formulate the strongest promise which A might issue in order to achieve its objectives. This promise can be maintained for an extended period, perhaps even 10 years or longer. Keeping it, however requires sustained effort by A and its allies. Keeping it is also dependant on the success of A to involve other states in the boycott and isolation of P.

promise

name basic promise of permanent pressure towards nonproliferation.

promiser A

body A produces durable pressure on P in a range of different ways, more specifically:

- A will systematically seek to inflict economic damage and distress caused by isolation on P, A knows that this policy depends on maintaining the support of a number of potential trade partners of P,

- A wants to see a change of behaviour of P, and does not care about a regime change, A is uncommitted to the question whether or not a regime change inside P will be helpful for reaching A's objectives,

- A will together with B and C keep their forces at high alert and will perform regular and large scale exercises to make sure that military cooperation between A, B, and C is optimal during an emergency related to P,

- A will, in collaboration with B and C, systematically invest in the development and deployment of defensive weapons systems, with the intention to deprive P of any first strike capability (and thereby of any second strike capability),

- A will on the long run outperform the developments of P in all relevant parameters,

- A does not publicly accept P's perception of the state of affairs as a phase of nuclear mutual quasi-deterrence and (though in private A may accept that very notion),[76] and moreover A does not accept the suggestion that this phase by taking longer

> improves the position of P, on the contrary, A will see to it that
> P pays a high price for each day it delays compliance with the
> requirements of nuclear nonproliferation,
>
> - A does not accept any preconditions in connection with putting
>   any of the above methods of placing P under pressure in ad-
>   vance of any negotiations with P. Such steps are only considered
>   once useful intermediate results are obtained during such nego-
>   tiations.

promisee P

negative condition P is not dismantling with its nuclear weapons, including its production facilities thereof and its related IRBM and ICBM
missile systems, in a complete, verifiable, and irreversible manner.

Qualifier +

deadline permanent as long as the requirements of nuclear weapons dismantling have not been met.

bias towards avoiding a nuclear breakout for P.

(hidden) source credibility $p = P_T(condition, B) = 95\%$

(hidden) intended target credibility $q = P_S(condition, B) = 75\%$
(this is the target credibility which A seeks to install in the perception
of P).

scope P, A, B, and C (that is the political leaders and citizens of the states
involved).

Once the basic promise of permanent pressure towards nonproliferation has been issued
by A to P, A may choose to add the following promise to it.

promise

name additional promise of permanent pressure towards nonproliferation.

promiser A

body A produces durable intensified pressure on P in a range of different
ways, more specifically:

> - A will regularly inflict minor provocations in the form of mi-
>   croattacks as specified in Section 9.1) on P so as to demonstrate
>   on a permanent basis that A is not fearful of P's responses.
>   These provocations include besides flights over P's territory
>   with drones and unmanned aircraft smal scale military attacks,
>   and covert operations inside P,

- A may without advance warning carry out (and support) covert actions against the infrastructure of P. Such actions may range from cyberwar to the denotation of explosives,

- A keeps open the option at any time to issue the following conditional threat in a final attempt to avoid an all out war, which undoubtedly will be very costly for A, just as for P.

  name embedded conditional threat of a first strike.

  source A

  body A will attack P by all means and with first counterforce strike intentions.

  target P

  condition P is not dismantling with its nuclear weapons, including its production facilities thereof and its related IRBM and ICBM missile systems, in a complete, verifiable, and irreversible manner,

  deadline 14 days.

  bias towards avoiding an all-out nuclear war with P while optimising (by showing military strength and determination) the probability that nuclear break-out for P is prevented.

  (hidden) source credibility 10%

  (hidden) intended target credibility 90%.

  scope P, A, B, and C (that is the political leaders and citizens of the states involved).

- A will not promise to P or to any other state or combination of states that it will not carry out a full fledged first strike against P, (thereby A creates a risk for P without even issuing a threat).

Qualifier +

promisee P

condition P is not dismantling with its nuclear weapons, including its production facilities thereof and its related IRBM and ICBM missile systems, in a complete, verifiable, and irreversible manner,

time span permanent as long as the requirements of nuclear weapons dismantling have not been met.

bias towards avoiding a nuclear breakout for P.

(hidden) source credibility $p = P_T(condition, B) = 75\%$

(hidden) intended target credibility $q = P_S(condition, B) = 50\%$ (this is the target credibility which A seeks to install in the perception of P).

scope P, A, B, and C (that is the political leaders and citizens of the states involved).

CHAPTER 11

GAMIFICATION FOR WAR: CAN THE WEAKER SIDE WIN?

In this Chapter I will proceed with the exposition of promises and threats for strategy specification. The problem for which I intend to suggest a solution is how to make use of promises and threats in such a way that it becomes possible for the weaker side to win the conflict without fighting a highly expensive war. This is a problem because by definition the stronger side will not see much incentive to give up its quest. I will suggest realistic gamification as a means to have bring the conflict to an end with minmal collateral damage and in such a manner that the probability of victory for either side is close to what would happen in a real war. Promises (rather that threats) will be used for the specification of realistic gamification.

11.1 GAMIFIED BATTLE, GAME, DUEL, CONTEST, MATCH, SUBSTITUTE BATTLE

I will be looking at ways to turn what might be a war into a contest where the stronger side may win without any side running the existential risks of a full-fledged war. This is not primarily a matter of recognising gaming aspects in a specific political setting but rather a matter of changing modes of operation into a confined setting, comparable to a classical duel between conflicting persons, or a sports match, or a beauty contest, or any substitute fight or battle which takes place in a setting that has been agreed upon in advance by both sides and which has been designed to protect as many agents as possible from adverse impact.

Nevertheless, one may recognise some gaming in any asymmetric case case, in particular a form of the prisoner's dilemma. Both sides may choose to perform a nuclear attack on the opponent without any form of advance cooperation. Avoiding such a course of events though, is profitable for both sides. Axelrod 1967 [3] states:

> The general hypothesis for Prisoner's Dilemma games is quite simple: if
> two Prisoner's dilemma games are played under similar conditions and
> differ only in their payoff matrices, then it is more likely that the players
> will make a noncooperative choice D in the game with the greater conflict
> of interest.

By casting a potential conflict in a in a confined space of operational options (realistic battle gamification) the size of the conflict may be reduced and the likelihood of finding a cooperative way of proceeding may be enhanced.

11.2　Victory for the Weaker Side

For A it is obvious when its strategy towards containment of the nuclear-weapons state ambitions of P has been successful. That is the case if P effectuates a complete, verifiable, and irreversible military denuclearisation. This aspect has been captured adequately by the conditional threats and promises as were suggested for A in the preceding Sections. It is mored difficult to imagine a scenario where A fails with its intentions and where nevertheless an orderly end of the conflict is found and yet a highly damaging military conflict is avoided.

A major difficulty involved in coming to the conclusion that P rather than A has been victorious is that the assertion that P is capable of nuclear-weapons based deterrence against A consists of a combination of positive statements about capabilities of P and negative assertions about capabilities of A and its allies. Moreover this balance between positive and negative capabilities is continuously evolving as both siders progress with research, development, production, and deployment of weapons and weapon systems.

If A is under no circumstance willing to accept that its strategy has failed then P may have an incentive to issue a threat of an all out final, and probably suicidal, attack on A and its allies, in the hope that there is some chance that A will in the end accept its defeat and will return to normalised trade relations and ending the isolation of P. For P it is essential that it can terminate the conflict with A in a successful manner. By means of two draft promises which P can issue (as promises) at any time these matters can be adequately specified.

threat

name treat of final and desperate action.

promiser P

body P performs a "desperate" and maximally damaging first strike on A, B, and C (while consciously and openly taking the risk that P may be entirely destroyed as a consequence of the second strike of A with support of B and C).

promisee A

condition One or more of the following conditions apply:

- in spite of a clear invitation by P to do so, at least 1 year ago, A has not accepted the proposal as formulated by P and has not put forward any proposal of its own for a peaceful process along which P can demonstrate that it has acquired the level of maturity of its nuclear weapons, missile systems, and other delivery options, which renders A's objectives and demands on P futile.

- A and P have agreed in the past on a process of validation of P's claim that it has achieved its nuclear-weapons ambitions, and P has demonstrated that it passes the test, but A is unwilling to admit that it has been defeated (in frustrating P with the realisation of its nuclear-weapons state ambitions).

deadline 4 years after condition has become true, the threat is supposed to be challenged and its body is put into effect.

bias towards avoiding unending isolation and economic boycott of P by leaders of A who prefer not to take notice of the fact that P has been successful in reaching a durable nuclear breakout.

(hidden) source credibility $p = P_T(condition, B) = 50\%$

(hidden) intended target credibility $q = P_S(condition, B) = 70\%$

scope P, A, B, and C (that is the political leaders and citizens of the states involved).

11.2.1 PROPOSING A PROTOCOL FOR JOINT DEMONSTRATIONS

Agreement on a method by which P can demonstrate to A and its allies that it has achieved a mature nuclear-weapons competence can be found when A issues a promise of the following kind and subsequently P promises to accept that promise.

promise

name proposing a method for P to demonstrate to A (B, and C) that it has acquired a durable and effective nuclear breakout.

promiser A

body A will accept that P is a nuclear-weapons state for a period of 25 years, and A will lift boycotts and other economic repression in the direction of P, and A will not stand in the way of further nuclear weapons and missile development by P.

promisee A

condition The following conditions apply:

- P has been able to launch at least 5 missiles to isolated oceanic locations, with a precision of 1 km from the target location, where time and target location had been notified to A well in advance, so than A can prepare its ABM defense systems for this particular sequence of tests, and from these five or more missiles at least two have survived A's defensive ABM's systems. These locations are so far away that similar results with targets on A's mainland may be expected.

- P has been able to launch missiles with a nuclear warhead and to make these warheads explode at in intended and predefined height and at an oceanic location which has been agreed upon with A at least one month in advance. (Here it has been promised by A that A will not try to intercept these missiles.)

- P has shown the ability to manufacture bombs and suitable missiles in adequate numbers (say at least 25 weaponised ICBMs able to reach the mainland of A and at least 50 IRBMs able to reach C) so that it can attack at least 10 cities of A,B, and C in a first strike. This is demonstrated by allowing A to randomly select missiles from the stock that P has acquired and to inspect that these randomly chosen specimen are not decoys.

- P has shown the ability to move around and subsequently hide at least 25 of its land based missile launchers so that there is little doubt that A is nowhere near the capability to perform a first counterforce strike against P.

  The ability to hide the launchers has been tested by asking A to indicate the locations (with the territory of P) and by subsequently allowing inspections by representatives of A, B, and C on these locations.

- Any subset of the above challenges has been achieved which to the satisfaction of A demonstrates that P has become a fully operational nuclear-weapons state, this in spite of A's sustained efforts (made in cooperation with its allies B and C and other more remote allies, to prevent precisely that from happening).

deadline 4 years after condition has become true, the threat is supposed to be challenged and its body is put into effect.

bias towards avoiding unending isolation and economic boycott of P by leaders of A who prefer not to take notice of the fact that P has been successful in reaching a durable nuclear breakout.

(hidden) source credibility $p = P_T(condition, B) = 90\%$

(hidden) intended target credibility $q = P_S(condition, B) = 75\%$

scope P, A, B, and C (that is the political leaders and citizens of the states involved).

This collection of challenges to P by means of which it may prove to A that it has acquired a mature degree of nuclear deterrence against A is too simple for practical purposes. Additional clauses are needed when P fails one of the test and needs a "resit" and about how often A is supposed to cooperate in this kind of a joint effort. Additional information is also needed about the timing of various challenges.

11.2.2 Accepting a Protocol for Joint Demonstrations

The following promise can be issued in response of a promise proposing a protocol for joint demonstrations. Once both promises have been such such a protocol can be considered to be in place so that it can regulate further events.

promise

name accepting a proposal for a method for P to demonstrate a durable and effective nuclear breakout.

promiser P

body P agrees with a proposal made by A in a recent (and unambiguously known to all parties) "promise proposing a method for P to demonstrate to A (B, and C) that it has acquired a durable and effective nuclear breakout".

promisee A

condition P has received from A a "promise proposing a method for P
to demonstrate to A (B, and C) that it has acquired a durable and
effective nuclear breakout" and P agrees with the details of that
proposal.

deadline 1 year after condition has become true,

bias towards avoiding the incentive to carry out a first strike out of desperation.

(hidden) source credibility $p = P_T(condition, B) = 90\%$

(hidden) intended target credibility $q = P_S(condition, B) = 90\%$

scope P, A, B, and C (that is the political leaders and citizens of the states
involved).

The idea of issuing a "promise proposing a method for P to demonstrate to A (B,
and C) that it has acquired a durable and effective nuclear breakout" is that if A passes
some simple tests (as specified in the proposal) which need not lead to any civilian or
military casualties and which may not even lead to much damage it can be considered
a proven fact that P has acquired substantial nuclear deterrence against A, B, and C.
Once that state of affairs has been acknowledged by A, the states involved can move
from a problematic phase of disputed quasi-deterrence to a possibly less problematic
an certainly more well-known phase of mutually recognised nuclear deterrence with all
political consequences thereof.

Proposition 11.2.1. *Physical and realistic war game-like activity threads (perhaps best
understood as joint military exercises performed by the conflicting adversaries) may be
used to demonstrate the existence of a state of nuclear deterrence in either direction and
in particular in the direction which is being disputed, and thereby to demonstrate that
thinking in terms of wars must be henceforth avoided.*

Proposition 11.2.2. *It is useful and advisable for A to specify by way of an exchange of
promises a pathway along which A may acknowledge defeat. By doing so A reduces the
risk of P starting a destructive war out of desperation.*

11.3 POTENTIAL WIN-WIN SITUATIONS

In the previous section it has been outlined how exchanges of promises can be helpful
for creating a gamified version of a potential nuclear conflict. In the gamified version of
a war, the various parts of the game involve military exchanges that have been set up in

such a manner as to allow meaningful predictions on what the outcome of a full fledge war will be or would have been, thereby potentially rendering the real war useless and futile.

The gamified version of a conceivable nuclear war may be tuned in such a way that the probabilities on various outcomes are kept almost the same. Transition to a phase of gamified war requires that a win-win situation can be seen by both sides. The following elements may contribute to a win-win situation for A and P:

- For both sides preparation for a gamified war is much cheaper that for a real war.

- For both sides a gamified war reduces risks of large scale destruction.

- For both sides a gamified war will be much cheaper to conduct.

- With a gamified war the mysterious element of chance (of a war taking place), an aspect which permeates the literature on nuclear deterrence, and highly contributes to the difficulty of rational decision taking in case of stress, is made less influential.

- Embarking on a gamified war introduces a phase of planning and preparation which is reassuring and constructive. It may lead to useful spin-off results.

- A gamified war may be modularised in such a manner that the confusion of simultaneous surprises is avoided.

A major conceptual difficulty is that without a real war the outcome of a gamified war may in some cases be hard to find out. In particular if a gamified war leads to the conclusion that both sides avail of a second strike capability which certainly justifies the absence of war in the light of conventional nuclear deterrence ideas, then it is still open how long that equilibrium will last. Perhaps when concluding on the basis of a gamified war that having an actual war is not conceivably advantageous for either side, and by declaring the existence of an equilibrium of mutual nuclear deterrence a second round of these games, say 25 years later, must be planned.

11.4   DECLARATION OF CYBER WAR

Perhaps the whole idea of a nuclear deterrence can be abandoned in some cases by moving the war to different areas of technology. For instance A and P might declare a cyber war. Here are some potential steps.

Informational money only payments for P.
  A and its allies may try to convince the world that payments to and from P from now on must be performed by means of a specific informational money only.[77]

Taking Bitcoin as the informational money of choice may serve both sides in the conflict. For A the following advantages can be mentioned:

- Mining is very expensive so that significant participation in mining constitutes a burden for P.
- At any time Bitcoin may collapse due to technical or political problems.
- Bitcoin anonymity can be compromised.
- P will be more open to the Internet if it embraces Bitcoin.
- P may be handicapped by lack of access to state of the art computer hardware.

Advantages for P are:

- By redefining its economy in terms of an informational money P will over night become center stage in the world wide fintech development.
- P is guaranteed access to the Internet.
- Bitcoin is by now proven technology.
- P can operate with other informational moneys besides Bitcoin, thus putting in practice what it has learned.
- Investment in Bitcoin technology combines well with sustainable economic development of P.
- Working with Bitcoin-like informational money increases P's independence from legal systems outside P. The classification of Bitcoin in Bergstra & de Leeuw 2013 [11] as an exclusively informational money (an EXIM in the terminology of [11]) may serve as an argument in this respect.

Acquisition of new allies (both for A and for P).
When fighting a cyber war both sides may find and make use of new allies for their endeavours.

Understanding cyber security in military terms.
When a cyber war has been declared by a state, it wil be necessary to understand cyber security in military terms. This allows the enforcement of much stricter security rules than have emerged from commercial use of IT.

Damage control.
When declaring a cyber war it must be promised that the cyber war will not inadvertently escalate into a mechanical war and especially not into a nuclear war. It must be a rule that a step towards physical escalation requires the formal end of the declared cyber war.

A practice of cyber wars may lead to UN regulation. If a cyber war can be helpful to deflect and reduce the stress coming from a (structural) threat of a physical war, then the potential of cyber wars must be exploited and welcomed rather than avoided and disregarded.

Engaging in a phase of declared cyber war between A and P represents a next stage of gamification of the conflict. In contrast with a modular gamified war a cyber war cannot be used to predict the outcome of a "real" war.

CHAPTER 12

CONCLUDING REMARKS

As a case study on Promise Theory and its extension with threats the KCW is notable by the highly asymmetric military capabilities of the states involved. I have not paid any attention to the potential role of promises and threats in different highly asymmetric cases, for instance the case of one or more states confronting a nuclear-weapons grade terrorist group. As detailed in depth in Axelrod & Borzutzky 2006 [4] such phenomena need to be taken seriously by institutions which may be traditionally disinclined to do so.

12.1   ON THE MENU OF POTENTIAL ACTIONS

In order to assess the relative importance of promises and threats (in the context of a potential military conflict) these must be understood as options within a larger pool of potential actions. Here is a listing of such alternatives as may be contemplated by a stronger side A against an allegedly weaker side P.

Redistributing troops and equipment.
> Movements may be within states, to and from borders, as well as between states, naval movements included.

Increasing or decreasing the power of weapons systems.
> Dedicated R & D efforts, increased production of weapons, purchase of weapons systems. Increasing radar satellite surveillance of P, and other satellite based intelligence methods.

Demonstrating the functionality of novel weapons systems.
> (nuclear) test explosions; ICBM tests, IRBM tests, ABM tetst, each of which may be conducted from a range of different platforms.

Visibly preparing for war.

Mobilisation of personnel and equipment. Transition to increased state of readiness.

Conducting military exercises.

Exercises range from small scale to simulations of a complete invasion into P.

Imposing trade restrictions.

Such restrictions require political work by A and its allies in an international context.

Imposing travel restrictions.

Travel to and from P may be partially blocked.

Imposing financial restrictions.

Money streams to and from P may be intercepted, P's funds outside P may be block ore even confiscated.

Confiscation of goods.

In some cases P's goods outside P may be confiscated.

Imprisonment of persons.

Citizens of P outside P, may loos various degrees of freedom.

Enforcing land and sea blockades.

This comes close to military action.

Minor military hostilities.

Including overflight of P with drones and spying aircraft, (not including satellites), including systematically following P's naval units with hunter–killer drones.

Covert action inside P's territory.

Open ended options ranging from terror to desinformation.

Cyberwarfare.

Of increasing relevance. Usually not considered a military action, but that may change.

Promises and threats constitute an addition to this menu of options. Plausibly, however, a particular option chosen from this menu, is embedded in a combination of successive promises and threats towards P.

Upon contemplating a larger menu of possible actions for various agents, it becomes increasingly practical to make use of a theory of action. I hold that the theory of multi-threading for computer systems, for instance as formalized in [12] allows for a structured view on processes made up from actions which is sufficiently restrictive to provide meaningful insights in a political context.

12.2 POTENTIAL APPLICATION OF THIS WORK

Additional insights in the logic and structure of promises and threats, which constitutes the intended outcome of this monograph, may be of use to any party in any conflict in which such utterances play a role. There is an asymmetry, however, as the side which is much stronger in military terms may be more in need of the flexible use of promises and threats than the other side. An important caveat, however, is that when a phase of negotiations arises the usefulness of publicly announced promises and threats decreases.

Specifically for the KCW case I have drawn the following conclusions from contemplating the usability of promises and threats:

(Alternative) facts as promises.

> Key historic facts dominating the KCW are controversial indeed, and may better be viewed as political promises of (alternative) fact.

Focus on meaning of promises and threats taking due care for conditions.

> Conditional promises and threats must be examined with care. The logic of such conditions is often non-trivial. Simplistic interpretations may be avoided by properly appreciating these logical difficulties. For instance in Litwak 2017 [36] one finds:

>> After Donald Trump tweeted "It won't happen" in response to Kim Jong-un's New Year's boast about North Korea's emerging capability to target the United States with a nuclear weapon, former Deputy secretary of State Strobe Talbott tweeted the question, "Has our next commander-in-chief issued, 18 days before his inauguration, a pledge that the US will wage pre–emptive war against the DPRK"

> In Section 2.2 it was shown that the answer on Talbott's question depends on the precise reading of the quoted promise.[78]

The counter-intuitive logical complexity of nuclear deterrence.

> Powell 1985 [46] draws some rather non-trivial conclusions from his equally non-trivial assumption that the choice to make use of nuclear weapons by a state targeting another nuclear-weapons state, once that unfortunate event actually would happen, is more likely not to be a rational choice than to be a rational choice.

Irrational behaviour may be caused by fear, panic, hubris, arrogance, ill-understood ethics, lack of information, miscommunication, tunnel vision, lack of creativity, unwarranted optimism, or unwarranted pessimism or any other cause. Now Powell promotes precisely the irrational causes of a full nuclear war to central stage, thereby arriving at quite counter-intuitive, though yet compelling, conclusions.

I conclude from Powell's arguments that promises and threats, precisely by providing adequate means for communicating irrational thoughts and motives, have a significant role to play in the handling of a conflict between nuclear-weapon states.

Moreover, it appears that many comments regarding recent US policies and about US communication on its dealing with the DPRK, by complaining for instance that the US Government does in fact (but should preferably not) increase the risk of a nuclear war with the DPRK, have been written by authors who either are unfamiliar with or are unimpressed by Powell's analysis of the principles of nuclear deterrence.

If negotiations fail, or don't even take place.
Given a nonproliferation oriented conflict between two nuclear-weapons states, a stronger state A and a weaker state P, and in the absence of a negotiated solution (with whatever outcome), then on the long run, the promises and threats as discussed in Chapters 9, 10, and 11 may become relevant for A and P, and for their respective allies. This suggestion holds true for the specific case of KCW just as well.

Impartiality. Taking a focus on promises and threats appears to facilitate and ask for an impartial view of a conflict. Writing in impartially can coincide with choosing a position, though it requires an explicit attempt to hide a chosen position. An unbiased analysis is helpful for an assessment of the options for negotiated conflict resolution.

Waltz analysis may still be "state of the art".
Classical deterrence theory, as originally put forward by Waltz, does not explain why it would be problematic to recognise the DPRK as a nuclear-weapons state, on the contrary it suggests not to be worried too much about nuclear proliferation.

Promises and threats with limited scope: guesswork.
Promises with a very limited scope, e.g. the US government only, or the DPRK government only, have not been discussed here for the simple reason that I have no information about such promises. It is easy to imagine, however, that

promises with very limited scope play an important role in the unfolding of political processes.

12.3 THE END OF NUCLEAR PROLIFERATION?

By way of a thought experiment I will assume that (i) at some future stage nation states still exist as policy units while (ii) the process of nuclear proliferation comes to a halt. Moreover I will assume that (iii) states are left quite free in the development and deployment of conventional weapons systems. Finally I assume that (iv) some combination of nuclear-weapon states has promised together that nuclear further proliferation will be prevented.

I will now contemplate how this appealing status quo might have come about. Three scenario's may be distinguished regarding the way in which proliferation will terminate:

Diplomatic path.
> A preferable scenario is that through international negotiations and treaties all non-nuclear-weapons states that potentially aspire the command over their own nuclear weaponss are convinced that this ambition must not be put into practice.

Conventional wars.
> Diplomatic means to bring proliferation to a halt fail and one or more conventional wars are conducted in order to stop nuclear proliferation. These wars having been successful, diplomacy suffices thereafter to halt proliferation.

Nuclear wars.
> Counterintuitively a nuclear war may play a role in the final stage of bringing nuclear proliferation to a halt. This is the case if it is deemed necessary by proponents of nuclear nonproliferation to reverse the acquisition of nuclear weapons by one or more states. It is plausible that once nuclear weapons have been successfully used for this purpose subsequent arrangements will be made by means of diplomacy.

Now suppose that a state Q has been able to reach a stage of maturity from which it may, without further external support, develop state of the art nuclear weapons technology including effective means of weapon delivery.

Suppose that Q knows that a nuclear war to end proliferation will not occur, for instance because of a widespread agreement that for such a war the end does not justify the means. Then what stops Q from sprinting (terminology of Narang 2017 [40]) towards the possession of usable nuclear weapons? Either diplomacy or the threat of a conventional war must then contain Q's ambitions, but for a conventional war Q may already be quite well-prepared.

I infer from these considerations that ruling out in principle the nuclear war scenario for the final stage of bringing nuclear proliferation to a halt is a self-contradictory position for the leadership of the mentioned combination of nuclear-weapons states that intends stop nuclear proliferation.

In other words, inasmuch as the combination of states insists on the perspective that the conflict with the Q is about arriving at the endpoint of nuclear proliferation, with Q ending up, in that scenario, as not being a nuclear-weapons state, said combination of states cannot rule out in principle that it will need a nuclear war against Q to achieve the intended result.

It is tempting to read the DPRK for Q and to view the US as a leading member of the combination of states promoting the end of nuclear proliferation. Can anything be inferred along this path? I suggest these conclusions, each of which is related to the paradoxical nature of the conflict at hand:

1. Rather than portraying the DPRK as a rogue state to which a separate logic applies, the conflict with the DPRK can be understood as a thematic matter, a conflict of a certain kind, an instance of which which sooner or later was bound to arise, and which is deeply connected with the plurality of perspectives concerning the way in which nuclear proliferation may come to an end.

2. It is a meaningful thought experiment (for the US and its allies) to understand the DPRK not as a failed state on any account but as a state which is entirely entitled to the design of its own political structure. The state Q featuring as the focus of the above description of scenario's for the end of nuclear proliferation might just as well be an impeccable parliamentary democracy. Justifying a nuclear strike against the DPRK on the basis of a negative assessment of its political structure constitutes an oversimplification of a conceptual problem that needs to be solved first under the assumption that the internal political structure of the opponent is considered unproblematic.[79]

3. Those who require the US to rule out the nuclear option against the DPRK in a categorical manner at this stage can be suggested to consider the following question: under which circumstances, in the context of a conflict about proliferation, would you prefer the US not to rule out the nuclear option? A further question would be: how do you conceptualise the end of nuclear proliferation if the use of nuclear weapons on pathways to its termination are ruled out in advance?

I end with formulating a proposition which I have come to believe during the writing on this monograph:

Proposition 12.3.1. *The use and communication of promises, threats, and alternative facts paves the way for productively confronting political paradoxes at least as much as a focus on facts is supposed to do, and perhaps even more.*

12.4 THE KCW FROM 2018—2019

As far as the KCW is concerned this monograph contains a snapshot of the course of events in 2017 rather than an up to date view. For the purpose of bringing promises and threats into position as analytic tools, thinking in the past tense is an advantage rather than a disadvantage. On the other hand so much has happened in the context of KCW, and has been written about it, during 2018 and 2019 that it is reasonable to pay some attentions to these developments.

As events after 2017 I mention that the DPRK has closed nuclear test sites and has at least temporarily ended the sequence of test explosions. Further meetings have been arranged between the presidents of the DPRK and the US. Wanatabe 2018 [68] discusses steps taken in 2018 towards turning the armistice into a peace treaty, he also claims that self defence must not be considered the reason for pursuing advanced nuclear weapons capabilities in recent years because it is known to the DPRK leadership that conventional weapons will suffice to destroy Seoul. The paper also describes the development of closer ties between the PRC and the DPRK, and the many nuances of writing about the perspectives of cooperation and unification between both Korea's, as well as subtle differences in expression how the Korean peninsula may end up being a nuclear-free zone.

Cha & Katz Fraser 2018 [20] explain how, in early 2018 the US has become suddenly less belligerent in its external communications moving towards high level talks in the form of on or more summits between the presidents of the DPRK and the US. The paper is written as an advice on the US position during the first summit, which took place on June 12 in Singapore. They also state that Trump's behaviour in 2017 had been self-proclaimed madman behaviour. Further they expect the DPRK soon to be able to send nuclear missiles to the US, a state of affairs which they claim, requires urgent attention. They strongly advocate that the US places its policies in the light of non-proliferation. Zhang & Wang 2019 argue that while achieving full denuclearization of the DPRK is not an option anymore, achieving the dismantling of its ICBMs is the best remaining objective for the US. Suh 2018 [62] points out in detail the long term continuity of DPRK policy that eventually led to the mentioned summit. Yeo 2018 [72] explains why the PRC is reluctant to impose economic sanctions on the DPRK. Shin & Moon [58] survey the outcome of the June 2018 Singapore summit and conclude that progress of DPRK military technology rather than US pressure made this summit work, and that the rewards of it mainly serve DPRK interests.

Technology is moving forward as well. For instance Carr et. al. 2019 explain how neutrino detection can be used to verify that a reactor has been shut down as promised without the need to enter the nuclear power plan, thereby potentially removing resistance against such proposals.

CHAPTER NOTES

NOTES

[1] For a survey of this work as well as some extensions of it I refer to Burgess 2015 [18] and to the more technical, and thereby somewhat less easily readable, exposition in Bergstra & Burgess 2014 [8] and to Bergstra & Burgess [9]. Bergstra & Burgess 2017 [10] provides an extensive case study for Promise Theory outside the realm of informatics. It appears that Promise Theory is useful for understanding systems of animate agents as much as it is for specifying systems consisting of inanimate agents.

[2] I will use the abbreviation KCW for Korean Cold War in the sequel. I refer to Toyorala & Feffer [64] for the phrase Korean Cold War; Oh 2016 [44], however, speaks of a Neo-Cold War in the Korean Peninsula, assuming that the KCW has ended already. I will not touch any legal aspects of the use of force in the context of the KCW. For recent work on that matter I mention Torres Rojas 2017 [63].

[3] Opinions diverge, however, on the role which the successive use of these two weapons of mass destruction has played in ending WW II, ranging from (i) instantaneously forcing Japan to surrender to (ii) providing Japan with a honourable argument for use by the Japanese Emperor when communicating the Japanese surrender to the US which was considered preferable to prolonging the war in view of the Russian (then recent) declaration of war which made a defeat unavoidable. Immediate surrender may also have been an expression of a preference for a forthcoming US occupation over an otherwise unavoidable forthcoming Russian occupation.

[4] See Nuclear notebook *http://thebulletin.org/nuclear-notebook-multimedia* (retrieved September 26, 2017).

[5] For a historic survey of non-proliferation see Ruzika [50], where as a conclusion some doubts are formulated on the moral grounds for subscribing to non-proliferation, a regime which demonstrably protects the haves against interference from the have nots.

[6] Nonproliferation has been and is still an important UN endorsed objective. Convincing arguments against nuclear proliferation can be found in Sagan 1994 [51], who disagrees with Waltz 1981 [66].

[7] Achen & Snidal 1989 [1] provide an explanation why it has been difficult to find empirical evidence for the successful use of deterrence: successful use of deterrence must be understood by surveying events (wars) that might have occurred but did not. Systematically sampling such cases is problematic. Schelling 1966 [55] uses the term compellence rather than deterrence, Sechser & Fuhrmann 2017 [56] claim, on the basis of a survey they have made, that nuclear compellence is not a demonstrably successful option either.

[8] Jensen 2008 [33] indicates that besides external security threats also internal political movements and pressures may explain the determination of a nation to obtain nuclear weapons. I am uncommitted as to whether or not Jensen's analysis applies to the DPRK in particular.

[9] I will make no assumption on whether or not the US can or cannot achieve its objective of denuclearisation of the DPRK without making use of military pressure. According to Weissmann & Hagström 2016 [70] economic and trade sanctions imposed by the US and its allies will not suffice to force the DPRK to reverse on nuclear weapons development. These authors emphasise the necessity of financial sanctions in addition. Their analysis does not prove the need or use of military pressure, however.

[10] In this monograph I will frequently use propositions for concisely stating a position on conceptual matters. In many cases a proposition reads like a definition as it explains a notion in terms of other notions, in some cases it reads like an axiom by merely requiring a certain connection between several notions, and in some cases a proposition expresses a link (a derivable property) between notions all of which have been defined elsewhere in the text. By referring to the assertion listed as a proposition I prefer to remain uncommitted to the role (as an axiom, a definition, or a derivable property) of that assertion in any detailed setup of Promise Theory. I prefer not to speak of axioms (or requirements) or of definitions because in many cases there is no ground for taking precisely the formulation of a Proposition as an axiom or as a definition.

[11] In this monograph I will mainly focus on promises and threats regarding the use or non-use of physical force. Nonviolent promises and, though to a lesser extent, threats have played a huge role in the history of the KCW. The 1994 framework agreement for instance may be viewed as a composition of promises. Following Farago 2016 [22] non-compliance with promises as exchanged in that framework have explanatory value for the coming about of the current stalemate. However, I will not focus on promises such as these have occurred or might occur in treaties and agreements or in the diplomatic processes leading up to the design and confirmation of such international contracts.

[12] For a discussion of bias as a promise attribute I refer to Bergstra & Burgess 2017 [10].

[13] The concept of a promise may be compared with that of a car. When speaking of traffic on public roads and one may assume that a car is equipped with various lights and signals, with safety belts, and a tachometer, etc. but in its most rudimentary form a car need not be equipped with any of these. When speaking of an ambulance, as a specific type of car, several additional features will be expected. Thus the concept of a car comes with a level of abstraction, that is a collection of expected features, which may be tailor made for the specific context in which the concept is used.

[14] In the terminology of Powell, US President Trump has chosen to escalate via putting forward limited options thereby creating a spectrum of risk of a nuclear exchange coming about, with irrational behaviour on either side as the most likely cause of the outbreak of a nuclear exchange, and deliberately increasing the perception of risk by making use of said options. Improbable as it may seem, following Powell's analysis making use of limited options in the spectrum of risk may be a rational choice and may well be a more attractive option than the alternative option referred to as making use of limited options in a spectrum of violence, although the latter choice works under the assumption that the use of nuclear weapons can and will be avoided.

[15] I take for granted that these conditions can plausibly be met simultaneously.

[16] Here a counterforce strike is deemed moderately successful if it leaves the DPRK in a state from which any attack will at most damage the US but will not create an existential risk for the US.

[17] These sanctions were less strict than the US had proposed due to opposition by the PRC and Russia. In addition the PRC and Russia urged both sides in the conflict to contemplate their joint proposal: the DPRK stops further missile development and in return the US and the ROK abandon their regular joint military exercises (which the DPRK considers to constitute a security threat).

[18] Only by explicitly withdrawing this threat the DPRK can achieve a situation in which it can be forgotten. Withdrawal, however, may appear in various forms, e.g. by means of an official repetition again stated in conditional form.

[19]I view this value as a rather high probability for an imminent disaster thus indicating a serious risk to the US. I don't know to what extent such quantified subjective probabilities are used by the political actors involved.

[20]If, however the aggression is initiated by the US then China has promised to support the DPRK.

[21]In the late 70s in Europe NATO had become the weaker side, and nuclear deterrence supposedly prevented the USSR from carrying out small scale attacks.

[22]In other contexts Promise Theory may have explanatory merit and may faithfully reflect a volume of empirical facts. Some examples of such cases are given in Bergstra & Burgess [8].

[23]Speaking of promise logic instead of Promise Theory might perhaps be considered more informative or appropriate, but I will stick to the phrase Promise Theory.

[24]Several features will be discussed which seem not to matter in the case of nuclear deterrence, in particular immediate reward and immediate cost.

[25]In the terminology of object oriented programming, however, threats are best understood as a class extension of promises. The proximity of promises and threats is such that existing or forthcoming theory of threats may considered as part of (existing or forthcoming) Promise Theory. A significant volume of theory about threats has been developed within the are a of nuclear deterrence, see for instance Powell 1985 [46]. Those applications of threats are not based on and underlying account of promises, however.

[26]in our discussion of nuclear deterrence there is no role for the immediate promiser's bonus and for the immediate promisee bonus.

[27]A negative reward may occur if the promiser feels increasingly being overloaded with tasks.

[28]Writing "I promise f to the reader" instead of "f" is unhelpful as that would expand to "I promise to the reader that "I promise f to the reader" ", thus initiating a meaningless infinite regress.

[29]If in a shop the seller states to a customer that the price of an item has been discounted, implicitly the seller promises the willingness (to the customer as a promisee) to sell (to the customer) the mentioned item.

[30]For instance rendering the TICDT of Section 2.3 as an instance of madman behaviour and encoding that judgement in a meta-promise may be understood as turning a reported result of promise extraction from President Trump's rhetoric into a met-promise of an alleged implicit promise.

[31]Typically: if you have not paid the amount due within 10 days, you will be charged an additional amount.

[32]The enthusiastic organiser of a trip may promise potential guests that the weather will be perfect. Of course perfect weather may be useful for alternative activities just as well.

[33]If the police promises person P that P will be arrested when found, that a person who contributed in a major way to finding P will receive a premium, and that such is promised to happen within a specified range of jurisdictions, then the claim or objective (of the promise) is that P has been declared "wanted", and that the public has been asked to help.

[34]If a promiser issues the promise to visit a friend in order to please their friend (a positive immediate promisee's bonus) while the promiser knows that the promise is in fact deceptive, then the promiser may experience a negative immediate promiser's bonus.

[35]When a site claims that only authorised persons are admitted to it, by proceeding with logging in, a human client promises to be in possession of adequate authorisation. (If that is false the promiser can't keep the promise, if the human client knows that the authorisation is absent the promise is in fact a deception.)

[36]For instance (Authorities) A may promise citizen B that if he has another fight with his neighbour C, he (B and his family) will be removed from their home. This promise may qualify as a threat assuming that B is known to prefer not to be moved. Other neighbours may be in scope of this threat. Now it may be the case that C has regular conflicts with another neighbour B' as well and B' may value removal of

B upon a further conflict with C as unfair (holding C responsible for the conflicts rather than B) and as a weakening of their own position towards C. Then the threat is an implicit threat to B' as well. If, however, neighbour B' in scope of the promise has no problem with C, they may side with C and may applaud the threat having been made and perceive it as a promise to B' as much as it is a threat to B. If the latter is intended by A and if such a derived promise carries an obligation (for A towards B') with it such must be explicitly stated in a separate promise with source A and target B'.

[37] Relative cost and impact can be defined for promises as well but there is no use for such features in the current work.

[38] Suppose that a panicing father threatens to kill his own little child. Such a threat is very significant because of (i) the combination of the father's ability of keeping the threat, (ii) the high cost for the father when doing so, and (iii) and the highly adverse impact in the target, and perhaps to other persons in scope, when kept. Persons in scope of a significant threat are faced with a problem that ought to be solved, and need to act cautiously and deliberately.

[39] It seems to be in the interest of both source agent and target agent to agree on a model for the dynamics of trust in relation to promises being kept or not kept.

[40] The new threat is more likely to be challenged, and for that reason it is not valid to work as if the threat which has been replaced has not been issued and its replacement has been in place all the time. It may be the case that after performing retrospective replacement some "new" event (i.e. not labeled as such before the new threat was issued) of non-promise keeping arise which negatively impact the target credibility of other threats, thus potentially leading to an underestimation of current and future threat credibility ratios by the source.

[41] For instance if the threat (issued by state A) consists of attacking a specific missile launcher under command of state P which is positioned near the border of a state then the threat is effective if upon the attack taking place the response from P is proportional.

[42] If an airplane hijacker threatens to detonate a bomb in an airplane unless some prisoners are set free, the threat is also (but less) effective if the prisoners are not released provided not doing so has been a realistically contemplated choice made by the target who is fully aware of the potential (and probable) consequences of that choice.

[43] Promising a promiser in return of receiving its promise (say p) that its promise (p) has been understood as a threat, may by itself constitute a deception.

[44] A typical threat issued by a ransomware attacker reads: if you don't pay 50 BTC to the mentioned account before the end of next week some (or perhaps all) of your currently encrypted data will be lost. From the wording of the condition is already clear that this utterance is a promise which qualifies as a threat.

[45] For example for a person P, inhabitant of a certain city, the perspective of rising sea levels within a century constitutes a threat, indicating that P's investments in real estate in and around that city may be wrongheaded. The use of "threat" in Axelrod & Borzutzky 2006 [4] refers to what I call structural threats throughout their paper.

[46] Providing a convincing account of the interrelation of promise, lie, threat, and risk, each embedded in an adequate brand of subjective probability theory, is a challenge. I prefer not to view Proposition 4.10.1 as a definition in order not to suggest that having Promise Theory at hand by simply providing some additional definitions concepts like risk emerge in a systematic manner.

[47] For an account of subjective probabilities I refer to Bergstra [7].

[48] And in compliance with the tenets of Promise Theory as originally conceived by Mark Burgess for application in informatics according to which there is no need for a distinction between promise and fact.

[49]By definition with a subjective probability of 50% or more. It follows from the dogmas of subjective probability that a subjective probability of a factual promise is always known to the (human) source of a factual promise because it measures their own (subjective) uncertainty which they are aware due to the definition of the very concept of subjective uncertainty.

[50]The intended degree of damage to inflicted on B may range from total destruction in the sense of MAD (mutually assured destruction), to a more modern view of AD (assured destruction) which involves the (assured) degradation of the military, economic, and political structure of B from which only a very slow recovery will be possible, and only if other states don't interfere.

[51]In practice limiting the development and deployment of ABM systems.

[52]This means that once B has issued an "unconditional defensive limitation promise towards A", A will immediately begin with limiting its defensive systems in the promised manner.

[53]As an undesirable side–effect A of this promise, by keeping it, A also facilitates nuclear deterrence of other states than B towards itself.

[54]The intended degree of damage to inflicted on B mat range from total destruction in the sense of MAD (mutually assured destruction), to a more modern view of AD (assured destruction) which involves the (assured) degradation of the military, economic, and political structure of B from which only a very slow recovery will be possible, and only if other states don't interfere.

[55]According to Wilson 2008 [69] the existence of nuclear weapons arsenals cannot be simply justified by the assumption that it works for keeping peace.

[56]Events which took place within 2018 or later have not been taken into account.

[57]The US is unconvinced by the viewpoint of Waltz 1979 [66] that one must not be worried by the emergence of new nuclear-weapons states under the (for the US unconvincing) assumption that such states all comply with a similar political logic.

[58]In Schultz et. al. 2007 [60] it was stated that the acquisition of nuclear weapons by the DPRK, as evidenced by a (then recent) successful test, is problematic. Ten years later the US still takes this position.

[59]If that happens, will other NATO members be required (obliged) under the NATO treaty to support the USA, in the light of Guam being a part of the USA? As it turns out Guam has been excluded from this arrangement on geographical grounds and other NATO members need not act in support of the USA if aggression of DPRK towards Guam were to arise. Nevertheless the US might ask for support from other NATO members who the US consider able to provide such assistance.

[60]Lieber & Press 2017 [37] indicates that counterforce strike capability towards key nuclear-weapons states is slowly becoming a conceivable reality for the US. These views, as put forward in older work of Lieber and Press are questioned by Boyd 2016 [15]. Boyd considers a reliable counterforce capability which eliminates an opponent's ability to retaliate quite implausible. Instead Boyd suggest that counterforce capabilities are better not developed and much lower numbers of nuclear weapons would still guarantee effective deterrence. Critical in that perspective, however, would be that US leadership does not undermine the credibility of its use of that core of nuclear weapons, in order not to risk the loss of credibility that retaliation will indeed result after a hostile strike.

[61]This path requires consent of the PRC and may also require a policy which effectively guarantees the PRC the endurance of a reliable second strike option against the US, a theme emphasised in Lieber & Press 2017 [37].

[62]This argument has been taken from Fievet 2017 [24], which focuses on the extreme external pressures that have shaped DPRK policies.

[63]In recent work Shirk 2017 [59] emphasises the need for the US to finally engage in peace negotiations with the DPRK as an element of a much broader policy advice to the US.

[64] This view is confirmed in Litwak 2017 [36], who considers the DPRK to have become the 9th member of the nuclear club by testing a nuclear weapon in that year.

[65] Classical literature on nuclear deterrence seems to take the nuclear warhead delivery problem somewhat lightly, probably because in former years the likelihood of an airplane, while carrying a nuclear warhead, surviving defensive weapon systems was much higher than it is to date. When using nuclear deterrence theory from the 20th century, it should be kept in mind that in those years the very availability of a nuclear weapon implied that some means of delivery (by airplane) was available also, whereas nowadays missile mediated delivery is needed to acquire a credible second strike capability.

[66] The PRC is not a plausible target for DPRK's nuclear weapons if only in view of the DPRK's dependency on trade with the PRC, and so is the ROK because the ROK can be struck decisively and by means of conventional artillery against which neither the US or the DPRK are likely to be able to launch a successful counterforce strike.

[67] The DPRK is unconvinced (as of 2017) that the ROK plus the US can launch a successful counterforce attack (either conventional or with tactical nuclear weapons or even including tactical neutron weapons) against its array of artillery units near the ROK–DPRK border.

[68] Shen 2016 [57] uses the phrase regime chance for the political changes brought about by presidential elections in the US.

[69] See e.g. *http://www.independent.co.uk/news/world/americas/china-not-accept-north-korea-nuclear-weapons-state-ambassador-cui-tiankai-washington-us-a7949896.html* (accessed September 20 2017).

[70] These classical threats will be spelled out in some detail in Chapter 6 below.

[71] A previous US regime as the DPRK might prefer to say.

[72] Many other conditions can be imagined: unless P promises to release a specific prisoner, or unless P promises not to perform certain specified military exercises, or unless P promises to move its submarines outside a specified area, etc.

[73] Adversary states working in the stalemate of nuclear deterrence might also ask respective chess teams to resolve a conflict in a peaceful manner.

[74] How many observers are inclined to believe that Israel, a state which maintains a parliamentary democracy, could be forced to abandon its nuclear weapons systems under the mere pressure of boycotts, isolation, and scattered microattacks.

[75] Here it is assumed that A and P are asymmetric powers and that it is implausible for P to perform a surgical first counterforce strike.

[76] The theory of asymmetric conflict of Arreguín–Toft 2001 [2] analyses each of its scenarios under the assumption that actual fighting takes place. The very absence of military exchanges between A and P indicates the presence of some form of deterrence, however short–lived the resulting equilibrium may turn out to be.

[77] For informational money I refer to Bergstra & de Leeuw 2013 [11] and Bergstra & Weijland 2014 [13].

[78] Powell 1985 [46] (see also Paragraph 7.4.2 item 7.4.2) suggests that clarity about such questions may not follow from the classical theory of nuclear deterrence. The phrasing of the question itself is vague too: what means "to wage war" in this case?

[79] In my view the autocratic structure of the DPRK weakens rather than strengthens the potential of justification of a nuclear strike against it, just as it is likely to weaken the effect of a threat to that extent. The less responsible the population of a state can be held for the policy of its leaders the less justification for the use of weapons of mass destruction can be found. Another paradox: a dictatorial regime may protect its citizens against the fury of an ethically aware opponent in ways a democracy may not.

ACKNOWLEDGEMENTS

I have profited from a guest position at the Informatics Institute of the University of Amsterdam and the corresponding library access including the access to the comprehensive JSTOR repository. Moreover I acknowledge critical remarks made by Dawid Walentek (University of Amsterdam), and I have made use of critical remarks on preliminary versions of the work by Mark Burgess, as well as from sustained discussions with him about promises theory, and more recently about its extension with threats,

BIBLIOGRAPHY

[1] Christopher H. Achen and Duncan Snidal. Rational Deterrence Theory and Comparative Case Studies. *World Politics*, 41 (2), 143–169, (1989).

[2] Ivan Arreguín-Toft. How the Weak Win Wars: A Theory of Asymmetric Conflict. *International Security*, 26 (1), 93–128, (2001).

[3] Robert Axelrod. Conflict of Interest: an Axomatic Approach. *The Journal of Conflict Resolution*, 11 (1), 87–99, (1967).

[4] Robert Axelrod and Silvia Borzutsky. NATO and the war on terror: The organizational challenges of the post 9/11 world. *Rev. Int. Org.*, 1, 293–307, (2006).

[5] Glenn Baek. A Perspective on Korea's Participation in the Vietnam War. *Asian Institute for Policy Studies, Issue Brief*, 53 (1), (2013).

[6] David A. Baldwin. Thinking about threats. *The Journal of Conflict Resolution*, 15 (1), 71–78, (1971).

[7] Jan A. Bergstra. Adams Conditioning and Likelihood Ratio Transfer Mediated Inference. *Scientific Annals of Computer Science* 29 (1), 1–88, (2019).

[8] Jan Bergstra and Mark Burgess. *Promise Theory: Principles and Applications.* χt Axis Press. ISBN9781495437779, (2014). 2nd edition χt Axis Press. ISBN50104452R00188, (2019).

[9] Jan Bergstra and Mark Burgess. *Money, Ownership and Agency.* χt Axis Press. ISBN50065677R00171, (2019).

[10] Jan Bergstra and Mark Burgess. *Promise Theory: Case Study on the 2016 Brexit Vote.* χt Axis Press. ISBN9781974545339 (2017).

[11] Jan Bergstra and Karl de Leeuw. *Bitcoin and beyond: Exclusively Informational Monies.* *arxiv:1304.4748v3* version 3, (2013).

[12] Jan A. Bergstra and C. (Kees) A. Middelburg. Thread algebra for strategic interleaving. *Formal Aspects of Computing*, 19(4):530–548, 2007.

[13] Jan Bergstra and Peter Weijland. *Bitcoin: a Money-like Informational Commodity. arxiv:1402.4778*, (2014).

[14] Roland Bleiker. Dealing with a nuclear North Korea: conventional and alternative security scenarios *In Eds. Antony Burke, Matt McDonald*, 215–230, (2007).

[15] Dallas Boyd. Revealed Preference and the Minimum Requirements of Nuclear Deterrence. *Strategic Studies Quarterly*, 10 (1), 43–73, (2016).

[16] Remco Breuker. As *if* it matters: the past in the present in North Korea and elsewhere. Leiden University, Inaugural Address, (2017).

[17] Mark Burgess. *Spacetimes with Semantics I. arxiv:1411.5563*, (2014).

[18] Mark Burgess. *Thinking in Promises: Designing Systems for Cooperation.* O'Reilly Media (2015).

[19] Rachel Carr et. al. Neutrino-based tools for nuclear verification and diplomacy in North Korea. *https://arxiv.org/pdf/1811.04737.pdf*, (2019).

[20] Victor Cha and Katrin Fraser Katz. The right way to coerce North Korea. *Foreign affairs*, 97 (3), 87–100, (2018).

[21] Justin Chapman. For the US-ROK alliance: less is more. *Patterson Review of International Affairs* 14, 1–22 (2014).

[22] Niv Farago. Washington's failure to resolve the North Korean nuclear conundrum: examining two decades of US policy. *International Affairs* 92 (5), 1127–1145, (2016).

[23] John Feffer. Trump and the Geopolitics of Crazy. *Foreign Policy in Focus*, August 2017, (2017).

[24] Nadia N. Fievet. The Ultimate Rogue Leader in History? Kim Il Sung and North Korea's position in the international state system. Utrecht University, MSc Thesis, (2017).

[25] Andrea Futter and Benjamin Zala. Coordinating the arm swing with the pivot: nuclear deterrence, stability and US strategy in the Asia–Pacific. *The Pacific Review* 28 (3) 367-390, (2015).

[26] John Gerring. What Makes a Concept Good? A Critical Framework for Understanding Concept Formation in the Social Sciences *Polity* 31 (3), 357–393, (1999).

[27] Simon Gonsalves. Korea Divided: the Best Way Forward. *Laurier Undergraduate Journal of the Arts*, 3 Article 5, 81–94, (2017).

[28] Colin S. Gray. The Case for a Theory of Victory. *International Security* 4 (1), 54–87, (1979).

[29] Frank Harvey. President Al Gore and the 2003 Iraq War: A Counterfactual Critique of Conventional "W"isdom. *Canadian Defense and Foreign Affairs Institute*, (2008).

[30] Carl Hewitt. *North Korea Deal?*, (2017).

[31] Christopher W. Hughes. "Super-sizing" the DPRK Threat–Japan's Evolving Military Posture and North Korea. *Asian Survey* 49 (2) 291–311 (2009).

[32] Shephen Iverson. Stop North Korea!: A Radical New Approach to the North Korea Standoff. *Tuttle Publishing*, ISBN:9780804848596 (2017).

[33] J. Andrew Jensen. Nuclear Weapons Proliferation Theory and the Case of Iran. *Hinckley Journal of Politics* 9, 29–41, (2008).

[34] Fred Kaplan. Don't panic about North Korea. *Slate September 5, 2017*, (2017).

[35] Bruno Latour. *Reassembling the social: An introduction to actor-network-theory.* Oxford university press, (2005).

[36] Robert S. Litwak. *Preventing North Korea's Nuclear Breakout.* Wilson Center ISBN: 978-1-938027-64-2,

[37] Keir A. Lieber and Daryl G. Press. The New Era of Counterforce: Technological Change and the Future of Nuclear Deterrence. *International Security* 44 (4) 2–49, (2017).

[38] Andrew Mack. Why Big Nations Lose Small Wars: The Politics of Asymmetric Conflict *World Politics* 27 (2) 175–200, (1975).

[39] James Edwin Mahon. The definition of lying and deception. The Stanford Encyclopedia of Philosophy (Winter 2016 Edition), Edward N. Zalta (ed.), (2016).

[40] Vipin Narang. Strategies of Nuclear Proliferation: How States Pursue the Bomb. *International Security* 41 (3) 19–30, (1986).

[41] Barry Nalebuff. Brinkmanship and Nuclear Deterrence: the Neutrality of Escalation: . *Conflict Management and Peace Science* 9 (2) 110–150, (1986).

[42] Barry Nalebuff. Brinkmanship and Nuclear Deterrence: the Neutrality of Escalation: . *Journal of Conflict Resolution* 32 (3) 411–425, (1988).

[43] Mary E. O'Connel. What Trump really needs to do to rein in North Korea. *https://perma.cc/Q2GY-WPDG* (accessed September 26, 2017), (2017).

[44] Chong Jin Oh. Neo-Cold War in the Korean Peninsula: Rising tension between South and North Korea. *Review of International Law and Politics* 12 (1) 27–32 (2016).

[45] William. J. Perry. Review of United States Policy Toward North Korea: Findings and Recommendations. (1999).

[46] Robert Powell. The Theoretical Foundations of Strategic Nuclear Deterrence. *Political Science Quarterly* 100 (1) 75–96, (1985).

[47] Dennis Roy. Preparing for a North Korean Nuclear Missile. *Survival; Global Politics and Strategy* 58 (3) 131–154 (2016).

[48] Dennis Roy. Misunderstanding North Korea. *AsiaPacific, Analysis from the East-West Center* 103, (2017).

[49] Dennis Roy. North Korea Policy: Failure is the Only Option. *Asia Pacific Bulletin, Analysis from the East-West Center* 379, (2017).

[50] Jan Ruzika. Behind the veil of good intentions, *International Politics*, 55 (3-4), 369–385, (2017).

[51] Scott D. Sagan. The Perils of Proliferation: Organization Theory, Deterrence Theory, and the Spread of Nuclear Weapons. *International Security* 18 (4) 66–107, (1994).

[52] Gary Samore. U.S.–DPRK missile negotiations. *The Nonproliferation Review*, 9 (2) 16–20, (2002).

[53] David E. Sanger and William J. Broad. Trump Inherits a Secret Cyberwar Against North Korean Missiles. *The New York Times* March 4 2017 *https://cyber-peace.org/wp-content/uploads/2017/03/Trump-Inherits-a-Secret-Cyberwar-Against-North-Korean-Missiles-The-New-York-Times.pdf*, (2017).

[54] Thomas C. Schelling. *Strategy of Conflict*. Cambridge, Harvard University press, (1960).

[55] Thomas C. Schelling. *Arms and Influence*. New Haven, Yale University press, (1966).

[56] Todd Sechser and Matthew Fuhrmann. The Madman Myth: Trump and the Bomb. H-Diplo/ISSF Policy Series, *http://faculty.virginia.edu/tsechser/Sechser-Fuhrmann-H-Diplo-2017.pdf* (2017).

[57] Dingli Shen. North Korea, nuclear weapons, and the search for a new path forward. *Bulletin of the Atomic Scientists* 7 (5), 345–3347 (2016).

[58] Gi-Wook Sin and Rennie J. Moon. North Korea in 2018, Kim's summit diplomacy. *Asian Survey*, 59 (1), 35–43 (2019).

[59] Susan Shirk. Trump and China: Getting to Yes with China. *Foreign Affairs* 96, 20–27 (2017).

[60] George P. Schultz, William J. Perry, Henry A. Kissinger and Sam Nunn. A World Free of Nuclear Weapons. *The Wall Street Journal, January 4 2007*, P A15, (2007).

[61] Joshua Stanton, Sung-Yoon Lee and Bruce Klingner. Getting Tough on North Korea: How to Hit Pyongyang Where It Hurts. *Foreign Affairs* 96, 65–75 (2017).

[62] Jae-Jung Suh. Kim Jong Un's move from nuclearization to denuclearization? Changes and continuities in North Korea and the future of Northeast Asia. *The Asia-Pacific Journal*, 16 (10 no. 2 Article ID5144), (2007).

[63] Gloria M. Torres Rojas The North Korean Nuclear Crisis: an Assessment of the Legal Justification of the Use of Force by the United States. *Global Journal of Politics and Law Research* 5 (1) 15–25, (2017).

[64] Georgy Toyorala and John Feffer. The New Korean Cold War: Relations with North Korea have taken a turn for the worse, but there is also an opportunity in this crisis. *Foreign Policy in Focus*, May 6, (2009).

[65] Kenneth N. Waltz. *Theory of International Politics.* Random House, ISBN 394-34942-3, (1978).

[66] Kenneth N. Waltz. The Spread of Nuclear Weapons: More May Be Better. Adelphi paper no. 171 IISS, (1981).

[67] Kenneth N. Waltz. Realist thought and neorealist theory. *Journal of International Affairs* 44 (1) 21–37, (1990).

[68] Takeshi Watanabe. *The Panmunjon declaration for North Korea: nuclear weaponry, alignment, and regime competition.* National Institute for Defense Studies, NIDS Commentary no. 74, Japan, (2018).

[69] Ward Wilson. The Myth of Nuclear Deterrence. *Nonproliferation Review* 15 (3) 421–439, (2008).

[70] Mikael Weissmann and Linus Hagström. Sanctions Reconsidered: the Path Forward with North Korea. *The Washington Quarterly*, 39, Issue 3, (2016).

[71] Hongyu Zhang and Kevin Wang. A nuclear-armed North Korea without ICBMs: the best achievable objective. *The Nonproliferation Review*, 26 (1-2), 143–153, (2019).

[72] Y. Yeo. Why does China hesitate to impose economic sanctions against North Korea. Video presentation, (2018).

About the Author

Jan Bergstra is a Dutch theoretician in applied logic with a background in informatics. He is currently active as an independent researcher and consultant working within Minstroom Research BV, Utrecht, The Netherlands.

His research has focussed on logical aspects of theoretical informatics, to mention: term rewriting, process algebra, abstract data types, instruction sequences, proposition algebra, meadow theory, and informational money.

Since 2008 Jan Bergstra has been cooperating with with Mark Burgess from Oslo in the context of Mark Burgess' approach to Promise Theory.